SUPER2SCROOGE

3000 SNEAKY STEPS TO
AN EASIER LIFE

D1494032

What they said about SuperScrooge
or 3000 sneaky ways to save money

A guide to being unashamedly mean – *Daily Telegraph*

No sucker gets an even break from Malcolm Stacey – *Daily Mirror*

Delightfully irreverent and shameless – *Yorkshire Evening Press*

One wondered how he got so rich on a BBC income – *Loose Ends, Radio Four*

The perfect guide to urban survival . . . outrageous – *ITV*

You can tell this miser by the champagne he drinks – *Northern Echo*

How to get almost anything at half price . . . just what I want to know – *Derek James, Radio Two*

Makes Scrooge look like an amateur – *Grampian TV*

How can anyone behave like this? – *This Morning*

Brilliant . . . This will sell and sell – *LBC*

It costs him nowt to live like a King – *Daily Star*

The confessions of broadcaster Malcolm Stacey are not a pleasant sight – *Yorkshire Post*

Is this the cleverest man in Britain? – *Hull Daily Mail*

Mean Malcolm rounds up a fortune – *Sun*

A compendium of wizard wheezes on the art of luxurious frugality – *Bookseller*

The hard-up will find this an investment – *The Physiotherapist*

Meanest man in Britain – *Daily Express*

Who else would say a friend in need is a nuisance? – *Daily Record*

SUPER2SCROOGE

3000 SNEAKY STEPS TO AN EASIER LIFE

MALCOLM STACEY

Illustrations by Pat Drennan
with some by Richard Stacey

QUILLER PRESS

In loving memory of my mother Hilda

First published by Quiller Press Ltd
46 Lillie Road
London SW6 1TN

Copyright © 1992 Malcolm Stacey

ISBN: 1 870948 80-7

Category: Humour

Produced by Hugh Tempest Radford Book Producers
Printed in Great Britain by St Edmundsbury Press

Contents

Acknowledgements

Acknowledgements to those SuperScroogists who incidentally helped us coin our motto: *Quo veni donat assistum, arrestus nihil.* When it comes to giving help, stop at nothing.

Jo Perkins, Robin Thomas, Douglas Waring, Richard Fredericks, Kathy Fletcher, Lilian Watts, Marjorie Freemantle, Ray Tiffany, Joan Mitchell, Shirley Cummings, John Howard, David Berry, Debbie Thrower, Ken Vass, Johnny Dimmock, James Watt, Louise Beeston, Sioned Mair Trick and Helen Weaver.

Preface

Professor Stacey astounds us again. If his first impressive volume took money-saving to the edge, then this second work pushes a related subject, time and energy conservation, beyond the ultimate.

And for those who say the ultimate cannot be transgressed, I care nothing. For this is not a guide for pedants. It is aimed only at those with the imagination and insight to realize that a new life of luxury and ease lies within.

Yet the conventional world is not ready for these ideas. And as I am now high in public life, I must withold my name.

I first met SuperScrooge when he was a student in the West Riding's Harlequin coffee lounge. Even in those earlier days his promise as a manipulator of life's miriad opportunities shone through clearly enough. Many years have passed since the late fifties, years which have culminated in a masterpiece. You now hold it – and your future as a connoisseur of leisure – in your hands.

Anon.

Introduction

Time, like an ever-rolling stream, bears all its sons away
—*An old hymn*

DO you spend all your days wishing there were more than 24 hours in a day? Are you tired of running around at work, at play, in the home or in the shops, just to keep up? If you're on business and social treadmills with no time to stand and stare, then, in all humility, *SuperScrooge 2* is indispensable.

I can make this claim because the first SuperScrooge guide – *3,000 Sneaky Ways to Save Money* – had two strong consequences, not entirely unforeseen. Many readers found their average incomes began to go five times as far. They're now steeped in riches, the living is opulent. Good luck to them.

But perhaps more significant in the broader historical realm is that the book aroused so much interest; the publishers were soon awash in academic contribution and inquiry. We took the only responsible course of imposing a scale of fees for the extra administration involved.

And as a result we were able, even without our expected grant from the Department of Education, to install study groups in all regions – their one function: to research, develop and collate material for a sequel on saving time and energy. Many of these adjuncts to the SuperScrooge Movement were further reinforced by experts from my own family.

Of course, one can save both by buying slip-on shoes instead of lace-ups, eating from cans instead of growing your own vegetables, and running to work instead of walking. These actions may save a few minutes, but they will do nothing for your dress sense, diet or dignity. Nor will they enhance your social standing.

As we now have at our disposal some of the best time and motion economists in the country – to be known henceforth as Super-Scroogists or Scroogists – we decided on a more ambitious venture.

We briefed all 26 study groups and they came up with thousands of sophisticated yet practical ways to save time and energy – mainly, it must be said, by getting others to do the work.

Follow just a few strategies, none of which require practice, and you'll not only have time to smell the roses, but you'll soon enjoy a trouble-free life of ease and contentment. And if it's at someone else's expense . . . well, it won't be at yours.

At Work

Or What the Chap who Wrote 'What they Don't Teach You at Harvard Business School' Never Taught You.

How can I take an interest in my work when I don't like it?
—*Francis Bacon*

COMPARED to those finer things in life – staying in bed, dozing in front of roaring fires on frosty nights, gracing deck-chairs on cruise liners – there's no more criminal waste of time than going to work (film criticism and wine-tasting excepted). Not only are forty to sixty hours a week denied to us, but we're forced to misuse even more time getting ready, going to and coming back from it. And some unfortunates even take their labours home. It's unjust. Diabolically so. And that's why dedicated time-savers are particularly active while at work.

The Five-day Weakened

Begin by paring your presence in the work-place to the bone. This means arriving slightly late and going home marginally early every day. You'll also want to come extra late and depart very early occasionally, too.

However, an unsubtle approach to this kind of time-conservation can cost you promotion – or even your job. Luckily there are ways of implying that the most assiduous clock-watcher is actually a workaholic. I rely, of course, on Meyer's Maxim: Seen once, a hundred times assumed.

In context this means that, to allay any suspicions that you're not pulling your weight, you will, once or twice, have to turn up early and stay late. Once this inconvenience is accepted, you can now follow the classic advice.

9

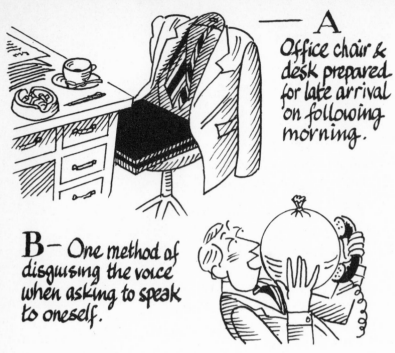

— A
Office chair &
desk prepared
for late arrival
on following
morning.

B— One method of
disguising the voice
when asking to speak
to oneself.

Very Best Ways to Hide Being Late for Work

Temporarily deposit your overcoat, jacket and briefcase in a neighbouring office before going to your desk. Colleagues will think you've been slaving away for some time.

Arrive with a tray of tea or coffee after going directly to the canteen. This is normally only done by people who've been at work for at least an hour.

The moment you arrive start ranting around the office. Threaten, 'I'll kill that spotty youth from accounts when he *finally* gets in.' This, of course, suggests you've been searching the building for some time.

Ring your departmental head in a disguised voice from reception. Ask if you can speak to yourself. If the boss grumbles that you're not in yet, say, 'Oh yes, he is. I spoke to him twenty minutes ago.' Recent studies (acoustic pioneers in Columbia) show that when masking a telephone voice, a balloon stretched over the mouthpiece is much more effective than the handkerchief so favoured by private eyes in 'forties films.

Leave a jacket or old handbag over your chair before leaving the night before.

If you have your own office invest in an automatic time plug. This can be set to extinguish your desk lamp an hour after you actually went home. It will also come back on again an hour before you arrive. The sliver of light under the door implies you regularly beaver away beyond office hours.

Intimating that You Worked Longer than You Did

The art of creating an illusion that you often stay behind to work late can't be over-emphasized. Yet regrettably we only have space for two devices here:

> Ring an unoccupied number (e.g. your sister if you know she's out). Ask in a loud voice, 'Hello, is Mrs Smith there? No, well please ask her to ring me back . . . [pause] . . . That's all right. I'll be at work myself here till at least 10 o'clock tonight.'

> Tell colleagues you're just popping out to the bank for a few minutes. For some peculiar reason people who 'pop out' are expected to come back. Break the mould.

Ways to Leave Early

Throughout this companion to modern Scroogism, you'll notice the use of accomplices is restricted, so reducing the odds of being found out. A rare exception is when you need to leave work early. For then it's best to have your excuse delivered by a third party.

Arrange for a friend (perhaps it's the person you're meeting) to call Personnel and say, 'It's Doctor Jones here. Can my patient [yourself] come to the hospital straight away? . . . Yes . . . I'm afraid it's about those X-rays we had taken.'

Should this lead to anxious enquiries about your health next day, you can look grave and say, 'I'm too upset to talk about it now.' Such a reply serves a double purpose as it helps you take even more time off later.

The alternative course, which doesn't require a co-worker, is nonetheless scorned by some of my students. They're unhappy on two counts: age (it was mentioned by Dickens) and its crudity. But why reject a ploy which is both simple and stands the test of time. It's known, technically, as timilation. In plain words: moving the office clock 15 minutes on.

Appointments with Fear

No one should feel guilty about making dental appointments in the firm's time. Canteen food is quite likely to have caused the damage in the first place. The same justification holds for doctor's appointments. Colds and stomach ulcers are more likely to be contracted at work. Even visits to the opticians could have an office origin: reading company reports can damage your eyes.

Consultation with Tabor's Tables shows the optimum time for all health appointments is 3.12 pm. A few minutes earlier and you might be expected to return to the office. Needless to say, you should only patronize clinics nearer your home than your office.

Cold Comfort

If your nose runs, however slightly, stay off work. Suppress any conscience twinges. Theoretically, if everyone with the snuffles isolated themselves in bed, cold and flu viruses would be extinct long ago. (How to catch a cold slight enough not to cause discomfort is explained in *Denzil's Unimportant Diseases* [Quiller Medical Library].)

Before telephoning to let the boss know about your indisposition, do a spot of screaming and shouting in a closed bathroom. A hoarse croak is *de rigeur* – certainly more plausible than a pinched nose.

It's also more convincing to ring in yourself, in an obviously distressed state, rather than asking your landlady or mother to do it.

A Back for the Future

Experts differ on whether back pain is eased by resting at home, or moving about at work. I know which school I favour. However, back twinges are rarely sympathetically received as a valid reason for staying away. So once again the most imaginative brains of our movement were consulted and they came up with a four-point plan:

(a) Come to work as usual.
(b) Half an hour later bend down to pick up a spanner or pencil.
(c) Cry out in agony.
(d) Be unable to straighten up till a colleague offers to drive you home.

Should you spot anyone else trying this gambit (Scroogists are everywhere nowadays) you should be the one to offer to escort them home. In fact, leap into the breach any time anyone genuinely falls ill or has an accident. Take your time coming back, if at all.

Ideal 'sprained back' angle.

Nobody Should Be Perfect

Letters should be brief. The more one-sentence missives you send, preferably in long hand, the more busy and hence successful you will appear.

Phone calls should be curtailed for the same reason. Winston Churchill was a master at this. When told that a German battleship was in the Channel he said one word, 'Why?' and hung up. This, he knew, was a more effective rebuke than losing his temper which always takes ages.

Winston was also making early use of a pure Scroogism. Always intimidate juniors with short barks during conversation: 'Yes', 'No', 'When?', 'Who are You?'.

How Not to Answer the Telephone

Am I teaching the sucking of eggs when I say the correct procedure in an open-plan office or workshop is always to let someone else answer the phone. Perhaps. But you may not know that the *Savage Study of Alternative Time Consultancy* showed that people who pick up phones work on average four hours harder a week, passing on messages, etc., than those who don't.

Occasionally, though, you'll want to pick up the receiver. You may be expecting a private call. If you're disappointed and the call is of a business nature requiring some action on your part, you should say, 'Sorry mate. I've only come in to fix the radiators. They're all comin' back in 'alf an hour.'

Most people who train with me are by now elevated enough to have personal assistants (be sure to call everyone else's personal assistant a 'secretary'). Your p.a. should block every call you get, while still eliciting a flavour of what the call's about.

Should the caller crave a favour you can forget it. But if he's worth talking to, wants to buy you lunch, say, you should ring back directly. This is more flattering than having your assistant act as an intermediary saying, 'I have a call for you.'

How to Save Time on the Phone

Should you call someone who's on another line, don't hang on. Ask her to call back. Of course the callee may not want to comply, especially if she owes you money or misunderstood you slightly at the office party. In this case leave your number not your name, and inform the receptionist that, 'If Mrs Brown would care to ring me back she'll hear something to her advantage.' As the poor woman will believe she's inherited the estate of a forgotten uncle a speedy response is assured.

If you're landed with a prolonged call from a bore – someone complaining about your company's service, say – you'll need to cut them off. Don't simply hang up. Instead start a sentence and bring the phone down half way through it. Then leave the receiver off the hook to make it look like a line fault.

A variation on this theme is useful if you can't get a word in. Suddenly start exclaiming, 'Hello . . . hello . . . hello . . .' – as though you can no longer hear anything. Then say, 'Damn' – as if genuinely upset – and bring the phone down.

Appearing Busier than You Are

The ploy of walking up and down, serious of expression, while gripping a well-stocked clipboard is too well known for serious consideration. Experiment instead with your in- and out-trays. At the day's beginning bulk out the in-tray with out-of-date memos and other useless papers. After two hours install all this rubbish in the out-tray. The cycle can then be continued next day by re-entering the pile in the in-tray.

To be really effectual the employer's attention has to be constantly drawn to the state of your desk. Cousin Barney's *modus operandi* was to label his trays in a comic manner so they became a running joke. Usually this entailed keeping three trays going, labelled 'In', 'Out' and 'Way Out', or marginally funnier, 'In', 'Out' and 'Shake It All About'.

Towards 5 o'clock you can consolidate your reputation as a fast and efficient worker by strolling towards the post room with what looks like a small tower of completed correspondence. In reality this is a collection of unused envelopes, which can be returned to your drawers for use the following day.

Sometimes an employee whose attitude is in the right place, but who hasn't studied with us, will be seen leaving in a lop-sided fashion as though struggling under the weight of a well-filled briefcase. A mistake! The chap without a briefcase is perceived as more efficient, because he retains only important information and can keep that in his head.

Side-stepping Time-consuming Jobs

When the boss introduces an idea which portends a lot of work for yourself, you'll need to put him off. It's no use protesting that you've already got enough on your plate. Here are some of our more useful counters (in order of effectiveness):

(a) 'It's a marvellous idea, even though it will be horrendously expensive.'
(b) 'Didn't Jenkins and Co. try that system last year. Yes, you know Jenkins, the firm who're laying people off.'
(c) 'If I remember rightly, the Inland Revenue got very interested when Smith Brothers tried the same thing two years ago.'

Of course, if your employer rather fancies Janet in accounts, you should say, 'Coincidentally that girl in accounts . . . is it Janet something or other . . . didn't she come up with a similar idea last week? Perhaps you should discuss it with her first.'

Pillaration

The odd name for this important weapon in the work-avoidance armoury will become apparent shortly. Based on that fine maxim, 'out of sight, out of mind', it involves choosing a desk outside the

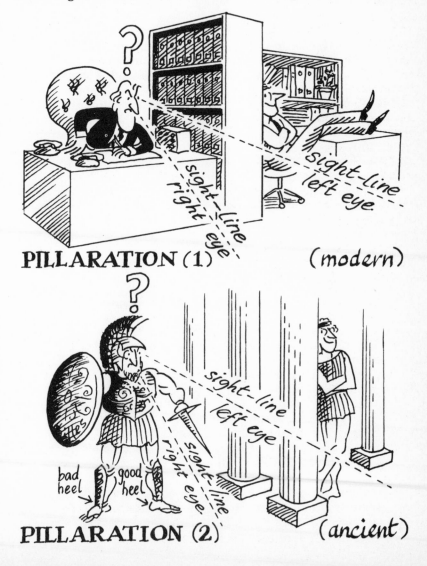

PILLARATION (1)   (modern)

PILLARATION (2)   (ancient)

boss's eye-line, i.e. behind the stationery cupboard or a tall filing-cabinet. If a job comes up it will always go to the first person of appropriate status that the employer sees.

The name 'pillaration' harks back to Ancient Greece. The story goes that when Achilles wanted a warrior to sneak unseen into Troy, Peronis lurked behind a temple pillar and his brother Telonme went instead. Telonme was pickled in boiling brine.

But for me, owning an inconspicuous desk isn't the entirety of this device. You must also be alert and, whenever in danger of crossing your superior's path, try to duck out the way.

The Secret Arts of Delegation

Managers find it easy to shuffle their duties onto underlings. Delegation is, after all, a form of flattery. Far from feeling put upon, minions are happy to be trusted with duties only an executive should safely undertake.

Robson's Business Guide quotes this example of a crafty delegator at work: 'Mrs Brown, I'd like you to work on the shift rotas from now on. I had thought of Mr Jones, but it really is *your* particular strength, isn't it – organizing people?'

Notice how the flattery quotient is doubled by comparing Mrs Brown with the unstated inferiority of a colleague.

It's possible, in fact quite common, for wily bosses to divest themselves of their entire workload this way. But you don't have to be in top management to delegate.

Indirect Delegation

To burden fellow workers with an onerous task you've been given takes more skill than direct delegation, so thank goodness for the 'I'll help you' dialogue. It works like this:

Supposing your employer has asked you to arrange a cocktail party for customers. The first step is to gather together a few colleagues for a quick word.

You begin, 'We've been asked to throw a party for clients in the board room. John, have you any suggestions?'

John the victim: 'You ought to get the wine from Sam's Off-licence. They do a very nice sparkling wine just like champagne.'

By saying, '*You* ought,' John still thinks he's only giving helpful suggestions. But you can turn this round and secure his direct help by replying, 'Right, I'll help you do that. Can you collect it in your van?'

By making the apparently thoughtful offer, 'I'll help you', you've switched responsibility for the supply of drinks to him. By asking, 'Can you collect it?' you've set the seal on John's total involvement.

Despite your vague offer to help, you can now fade from the

drudgery of buying and fetching drinks altogether. And similar routines can be worked to duck out of all the other party arrangements – from catering to hanging up coats.

This technique, which boils down to using the word 'you' instead of 'me' in negotiations, is sometimes known as Melton's Mulberry Bush, so called because you lead your fellows round the back of the bush, but you're nowhere to be seen when the procession comes out the other side.

Exploiting Newcomers

A more crude but nevertheless effective way of getting colleagues to work for you relies on the natural timidity of trainees. In my office it takes about four weeks for a youngster on 'work experience' to build up enough confidence to refuse to collect cups of tea or even go shopping for established members of the firm. When asking these favours it pays to seem extremely friendly. Newcomers always need friends.

Tricking a Junior Colleague into Working Harder

The merit of getting your underlings to do that little bit more is: (a) to take the strain from yourself; and (b) to win you extra kudos. Obviously a bald request for more productivity is too heavy an implement, but there are, as always, more inventive ways.

As soon as your minion shows up say, 'You're looking very tired this morning. Are you alright?' This simple question has a curious consequence, especially on older employees. They feel bound to work better and harder all week to counteract any suspicion that their evenings are so dissolute that they can no longer cope.

This effect, so satisfyingly out of proportion to the query put, can be bolstered by taking an inquisitive glance at the victim around lunchtime. The timing at around 0.7 of a second is important.

But on no account ask your question in a tone which suggests illness, as the powers of auto-suggestion may come into play causing the victim to go off sick.

When giving your assistant a routine chore, it's never wise to preface it by, 'There's not much to this. It won't take you very long.' Rather you should treat the task as an awesome challenge. Say, 'This is rather tricky. It's going to take a lot of hard work to pull it off, I'm afraid.'

The underlying psychology here is that the employee will begin to think there's more to his mundane brief than meets the eye; further, that his career somehow hangs on how well he performs. He'll begin to look for different ways of doing it better. You can then naturally claim any innovations that are discovered as your own.

Another way to rattle your assistant is to glance at your watch halfway through one of his tasks, so indicating that he seems to be taking rather a long time. A watch placed imperceptibly further up the wrist than normal makes this move more conspicuous.

Knight Errands

People with large companies find other opportunities to exploit workmates – by using them as unwitting errand boys and girls. If you have to deliver letters to the post room, remove them from your out-tray and leave them in someone else's.

Or if you see another employee loaded with letters moving in the direction of the post room, simply ask if they would mind taking your mail there too. Cups of coffee and sandwiches can be fetched from the canteen for you in the same way.

Keeping Meetings Short

We all know office meetings are a monumental waste of time. Yet SuperScrooge science allows the initiated to cut them short, and more, do away with the prolonged research needed to show you know what you're talking about.

Cousin Barney's artifice, which he calls the meeting-buster, makes a worthy place to start. He advises that when your turn comes to speak you must be taken ill.

This doesn't mean grabbing your chest and slumping forward. Such dramas are always unconvincing. Simply stop mid-sentence and look tense. Hold the pose for ten seconds. Then say in a rather matter-of-fact way, 'I feel very queer.' As all business folk live in fear of heart attacks, perforated ulcers and strokes, there'll be a rush to bundle you out of the building and into a taxi home.

Naturally, one can only try this effective manoeuvre once. So here, from the 1984 SuperScrooge Report (Interim) are a few other ways, all proven in practice, to keep a meeting brief:

> Install a selection of uncomfortable unpadded chairs around the conference table. It's also edifying to know that seats which are too low rapidly cause the neck to ache.

> Arrive early and turn off the radiators. No one lingers if it's cold.

> Phone through an anonymous cancellation of the standing order for coffee and biscuits. Many of your colleagues will be addicted to caffeine. Thus deprived they'll want to bring proceedings to a speedy close.

> Accidentally overlook two items on the agenda by going from number five, say, to number eight. Most of those present will also want to keep the meeting short and will pretend not to notice.

Ostentatiously gather together your papers and put your pen away before the last two items of business.

Instant Shorthand

Not a Scroogism in the accepted sense but still useful for those who strive to keep office effort to a minimum. This also does away with long evening classes on Pitmans.

Instant shorthand is achieved by writing normally without vowels, e.g. 'Y cn wrt shrthnd witht vwls.' The process can be accelerated by using t instead of the, tt for that, tr instead of there, and so on. Use initials for common phrases like itc for 'in this country'. Capital initials should also be employed for proper names, e.g. M sys tt F thnks T is rnd t bnd.

Instant shorthand is also used for insulting colleagues, even superiors, by leaving messages, which, because there are no vowels, could either read as praise or abuse.

For speed reading of company reports and an easy way to remember telephone numbers see the chapter on Leisure.

The Language of Commerce

Despite urgings of the Department of Trade and Industry, many companies have managed to forge no links whatsoever with Europe. Some weird and wonderful foreign legal and tax systems put them off – as do some weird and wonderful foreigners. Still, directors like to think they'll go international in the future. So it'll help your career to have several languages on tap.

Of course learning any new lingo serves no practical purpose whatsoever, as most foreigners of any importance can speak English. So wasting hours of study isn't recommended.

All you really need to impress the management is a light knowledge of accents (obtainable from BBC World Service or some Peter Sellers records). Then you can dial the speaking clock and talk gibberish in Italian, French or German style to a fictitious foreign customer.

Make sure there's no clever Dick familiar with the chosen language hovering near.

Instant Qualifications

May I now add a few niceties aimed at gaining professional respect without the need for years of tedious scholarship. In my study there are three framed certificates to impress clients. Hung fairly high to discourage close scrutiny, they seem to proclaim that I've won special diplomas as a consumer journalist.

The nearest document is unreadable as it's in Bulgarian. It certifies that I once had a ski-ing holiday behind the iron curtain (where ski passes are cheaper). The other two diplomas proclaim that, at the age of nine, I swum a length in breastroke, and that my house has been protected for fifteen years against woodworm.

Because, in 1967, I took fourth prize for exhibiting the most fragrant rose at the village show, I also refer to myself, quite correctly, as an award-winning journalist.

How to Be an Instant Linguist

There are, for the beginner, a host of easier ways catalogued for professing you're bristling with language skills, without undertaking the tedious preliminaries. Just a few of the most popular follow:

Leave a French or Arabic newspaper on your desk.

Enliven company reports with the odd French or Italian phrase, culled from a language dictionary.

Write to the Russian Embassy with some routine inquiry, about the August rainfall in Moscow, say. Ask for a reply in their language as you want to show it to a friend who's originally from Siberia. You will then have a letter in Russian addressed to yourself which you can leave lying about.

How to Get a Reluctant Customer to Sign an Order

Nothing heightens your standing as an employee or improves your profits as a manager more than the ability to persuade clients to sign contracts or orders which are not to their advantage. Yet, discouragingly, conventional text-books insist that a deep knowledge of your potential customer gleaned by extensive research is the only way to make a sale.

May I disagree and commend instead a trouble-free method based on a parallel technique I've encountered as a radio journalist? It's known as The Bumble.

When carrying out an interview with a fraudster who deserves exposure, one gives a preliminary outline of the questions. This introduction is full of mispronounced words, geographical errors, dropped h's, coughs and sneezes, ums and ers, banal repetition and general uncertainty about the subject in hand. So when the interview starts proper the interviewee is over-confident and off his guard. He sees no danger. He believes he can't be put on the spot or taken advantage of by an inferior person who seems to be suffering early senility.

This technique can be adapted to contract-signing. When presenting the document to the client, fumble and drop it on the floor. Have difficulty picking it up. Pretend you can't understand the legal jargon, and offer him a pen which doesn't write. Adopt the pretence that it's leaked ink all over your suit lining. The client will soon conclude that it's not worth reading the small print because you're simply not capable of guile.

The Correct Way to Dispose of a Boss who Expects Diligence

These careerists are a menace. They may use weaker variants of some of my tactics, outlined earlier in this chapter, for forcing minions to work hard. It's moral blackmail, of course, and very unpleasant.

A natural course is to complain bitterly about this obnoxiant to all who'll listen. How wrong! You must follow at all times the contrary principles of what's become known as William's Wangle.

Broadly this means amplifying the praises of your tormentor whenever you can – at meetings, in the canteen or in the pub. Make sure, for example, that the directors get a complimentary earful at office parties. This will eventually get the miscreant promoted into another department. (Two months from the beginning of your campaign is about the norm here.)

But William's Wangle doesn't stop there. It contrives to get the

WILLIAM'S WANGLE
Helping a troublesome colleague to rise like a rocket...

person head-hunted and probably out of your hair for good. Two connivances are possible:

(a) An anonymous news item is sent to the appropriate trade magazine. 'Rising like a rocket is Carol So-and-So of Amalgamated Rhubarb Chunks. At the age of 34, both ambitious and mobile, this human dynamo seems poised to take the fruit packaging world by storm. . . .' A rival company may well take the bait and put in a lucrative offer.

If they don't you should try:

(b) Sending a note to the managing-director of a big firm in the same field.

> Dear Bill,
>   Will call in the next few weeks with details of great deal we could do on bananas from Chile. All the omens are right. A modest outlay and we'll be quids in.
>   Kind regards,
>   Mike
>
> PS   Look out for that whiz Carol Smith of Amalgamated RC. You could use someone like her. Brilliant.

End with an illegible signature, which is nothing like your own. You can safely gamble that everyone in business knows more than one Mike. So if the rival MD asks one of his 'Mikes' about this letter and gets a blank stare, he won't be too puzzled.

Sadly, even the best of Scroogisms have their occasional drawbacks. In this case your head-hunted enemy will probably draw a better salary from now on thanks solely to your efforts. But at least she'll be out of your way.

How to Succeed at Job Interviews Without Preparation

I can't begin to count the days I've wasted studying and being interviewed for jobs I didn't get. That is until I learned the *real* secrets of securing a plum post. As suspected, there are no connections with ability.

No figures are available for the commercial world, but the following plan of action has to date resulted in 376 senior appointments in public service:

Begin by asking the personnel officer if he can show you round a week before the interview. Chat to people as you tour the premises. Be extremely pleasant. Drop clues into your conversation which make it obvious you'd be a very worthwhile colleague to have. These remarks should have nothing to do with professional competence, but be relevant to your social usefulness. Try:

'I used to be in the off-licence trade and can still get whisky and gin at half price.'

Or:

'Even though my mum's retired from the rag trade now, she still gets really nice stuff wholesale.'

Or:

'My father-in-law trains horses and, boy, is he in the know!'

Even if you can't impart these titbits directly to the executives who'll be interviewing you, the rumours will circulate ahead.

Another purpose of the pre-tour is to suss out the boss's hobbies or, with a bit of luck, her obsessions. You'll have time to look up the finer points of these activities in the local library. You can then drop learned references to these subjects during the interview.

Never criticize the firm you hope to join at the interview. Always understate your abilities and smile pleasantly. It's dishonest, of course, to exaggerate qualifications, but I see no harm in mentioning a day out you may have had in one of our cathedral cities. Perhaps you may be asked about your hobbies. A purely innocent reply might be, 'When I was at Cambridge, I became very interested in cycling.'

A useful ploy is to let the board think that they've already given you the job. An example of the technique is to ask towards the end, 'Can you let me know when I start?'

The Fast Way to Rise Within the Job

Those unfortunates who never avail themselves of our art patiently wait years for promotion, only then to be considered too old. Here's how to rise like a rocket:

Never underestimate your sex appeal. Meaningful eyes with short skirts or tight trousers work wonders.

Do a lot of after-work drinking with your superiors. See them home when they fall down.

Identify your main rivals for advancement. Be considerate enough to keep your superiors posted on their domestic problems.

Encourage your rivals in any daft ideas they have, and gently mock, when appropriate, their more promising brainwaves.

Leave an open memo on the competition's desk saying, 'A policeman called for you this morning. I hope it's nothing serious.' Another discrediting device to place on their desk is a bulky plain brown envelope marked, 'For serious art students only.'

Your firm is seeking a new executive and advertises the post internally. Type a letter on the company's headed notepaper, purporting to be from the personnel department. Make it appear that the interviews are a formality and you've more or less been appointed already. Leave this lying around your desk to discourage rivals.

Conclusion

There's no doubt that this is among the most fundamental of our chapters. The many stratagems, if correctly applied, will replace drudgery with contentment. Paradoxically you can do less work at your place of work than almost anywhere else. As Uncle Ernest, a key member of our work study group, puts it, 'All Scroogists simply love work – they could watch it all day.'

A Good Night Out

You have only, when before your glass, to keep pronouncing niminipimini – the lips cannot fail of taking their plie.
—*John Burgoyne (1722–97)*

M ANY a fine night on the tiles is compromised by time-wasting distractions. These include striving to park, waiting for service, battling against surly crowds, kicking heels at box offices and so on – delays which threaten a magical evening by inducing bad temper and indigestion.

Think how much more satisfying your expedition would be without the hanging about. There'd be more merriment, more wit, more scintillating conversation, more drinking done. You'd have extra time to impress on everyone what a vibrant, waggish, fascinating jewel of a person you are.

Thankfully, our socio-experts have been diligent. We're already in a position to present the results of their research.

The Marie Celeste Tendency

A most irritating drain on time is caused by pub owners and managers saving a few miserable pounds by failing to hire enough staff to work the pumps. The phenomenon, hardly discernible on Monday lunchtimes, reaches new heights on busy Saturday evenings. Yet who can afford to squander serious quaffing time? It follows therefore that quality cunning is required to beat that inevitable three-tier bar-room crush.

How to Get Served First at the Bar (Beginner's Sample)

Exploit your sex appeal. Women smile beatifically at the barman, men at the barmaid. Make your eyes smoulder, your lips moist. Perhaps the slightest suggestion of a wink. It helps if your choice is unattractive.

Hold out one £1 coin. The server will think yours is a very light order. Laziness dictates that you'll be dealt with first.

Say loudly to one of your party, 'We might as well stay here, even if they are selling half-price drinks at the Red Lion.'

While waiting, rattle a handful of change. Bar staff hate dealing with bank notes. It calls for skill in subtraction. Few have it. If you're without change, keep your folding money out of sight.

Increase the chances of rapid service by stationing different members of your party along the bar. Once one order is taken, the others can retire.

Rapid Bar Service (Advanced)

This list, though substantial, does not exhaust all the possibilities listed by our Licensed Victualler section. Here are the 'edited highlights'.

Noisily crash through pub doors while supporting one of your party who's in a collapsed state. Explain that she was almost squashed by a lorry. She urgently needs a reviving drink. Complete the entire order at the same time. This is also a very effective sequence for securing a table in overcrowded saloons.

The 'I-sympathise-with-the-difficulties-of-your-job' approach has some force. It depends on a common occurrence, an altercation between another customer and the barman, however slight. You must show your support for the barman by tapping the side of your head to indicate doubts about his antagonist's mental state. This works particularly well if the customer's clearly in the right and not too well built.

Hobble to the bar. Stumble heavily against it. Breath in loud, short gasps while working your mouth. Grip the woodwork in a panicky fashion. But stay bright-eyed to suggest you quickly need a drink for medical purposes, not that you are one over the eight. Concerned customers will stand aside and invite the barmaid to serve you first. The usual variation on this is to wrap a bandage round your head with a spot of red ink impregnated in it.

Don't try to secure eye contact with a bartender. He's trained to ignore it. Instead take some documents from your wallet or handbag and pretend to be engrossed. Bar staff love to inter-rupt serious thought.

If the landlord, identified by a large tum, is within earshot, call to the barmaid, 'You look very relaxed tonight.' This will galvanise her into action.

Sway about dangerously. Leer into another customer's face. Start singing 'Show Me the Way to Go Home'. Bar people can't wait to charge across and recite their traditional line, 'I think you might have had enough, sir.' This is your cue to straighten up. Tell them in a clear voice you were only joking. And, now you have their attention, put your order in.

Suggest you are a famous person by priming one of your party to say, 'I enjoyed your latest film!' Then you can reply, 'Ah, but Mel Gibson's latest did slightly better at the box office last week.'

Even if you don't look like a film star, the barman will probably think you're a top director who deserves special attention. This ploy shouldn't be dismissed as far-fetched. I've lost count of the times it's worked for me. Indeed easily im-pressed pub staff have even been known to give my 'famous party' attentive table service all night.

Manipulating Bar Staff

As you're being served you should flatter the hired help to ensure rapid attention next time. Something simple like, 'I like the tie,' or, 'How's that for lightning service?' will suffice.

You could also offer a tip the first time you're served – though a trained Scroogist regards any resort to bribery as an expensive cop-out.

Of course the most effective way to conserve good drinking time is to get someone else to buy the round with your money. Try these excuses:

'There's someone at the bar I don't want to meet.'

'I just dropped a contact lens on my lap.'

'Isn't that Michael Caine/Joanna Lumley standing at the bar?'

Or:

I was banned last year and they might recognize me. Then we'll all get thrown out.'

These ploys could be classified as 'academic interest only', as my adherents and I are always capable of persuading someone else to buy our drinks with *their* money (see *SuperScrooge One*).

Getting a Stranger to Bring a Free Drink to your Table

In a crowded bar your pint of beer is almost exhausted. You may have to wait a long time before you're served again. One of my cousins (understandably he won't permit me to name him) has formulated the perfect solution to this commonplace problem.

He'll pick out someone who looks both well off and diffident, if not weedy. This person should also be making expansive conversational gestures. David (sorry D. – it slipped out) will then hold his glass four inches away from, and at precisely the same height as, the more animated of his victim's elbows. It requires no skill to make covert contact between glass and elbow with the inevitable consequence.

If the mark (excuse the colloquialism but there's no equivalent word) doesn't immediately offer to buy him another drink David, who's 6ft 4ins, does *not* loom very close to stare hard. Rejecting this crudity, he simply makes a show of trying to brush beer from his suit – even if none landed there – while looking very glum, as if he had an important date which has been jeopardized.

Bad Pub Advantage

The careful choice of a regular pub is critical for the Scroogist. To make it easier for him to buy a drink, push his way to the toilets and avoid a customer who may be after his blood he'll need to patronize an almost empty, unpopular bar. Once you've found such a venue, keep it uncrowded by telling everyone that the beer there is damnably expensive. This is not legal defamation ('Slander of Goods') as *all* beer is.

It's also interesting to note that buying full pints rather than halves all evening can save forty-five minutes on trips to the bar in a congested pub – the London group experimented with the theory on four consecutive nights.

The Bar Meal – How to Get Fast Service

The main reason why pub lunches are served faster than those in restaurants is that bar fare is usually microwaved. So too is food in restaurants, but here a decent wait is observed between order and serving, to imply their food is lovingly tended over charcoal by French chefs.

But even pub cooking can be pretty slow. Particularly when staff are more interested in discussing football, holidays and the latest baby than heating up a rubbery vegetable lasagne.

You *can* ensure a fast meal though by asking (in concerned tones), 'Do you think this will take too long as a little boy *has* to go to hospital by two o'clock at the latest?'

How to Choose a Restaurant Quickly

We all know how much time is wasted studying exteriors and posted menus as we endlessly trudge the streets in search of the 'ideal' restaurant. Yet who can tell what the food is like till it's served and tasted? If you don't already know the best in the area it's got to be a gamble anyway, so pile into the first place you see. If it turns out to be unspeakably poor you will at least have somewhere to recommend to someone you don't like.

Saving Time in Restaurants (both Elementary and Advanced)

There are occasions when we actually *want* to dawdle in a restaurant. We may have just parted with a fortune in the hope of a relaxed conversation over several coffees at the meal's end. Naturally, this is the *only* time when waiters make it clear, by rushing around in fashion normally quite alien to caterers, that they need to see the back of you quickly so they can skive off.

But normally, and particularly at lunchtime in a working day, waiters star in their own slow-motion film. Avoiding diners' eyes is their delight. Serving quite the wrong meal, then taking ages to rectify the fault, is a skill proudly taught at catering colleges around the world.

Fortunately for diners, the Scroogist is instructed in some counter-skills of his own, including a few ways to ensure a galloping, grovelling waiter service.

You can, for example, secretly filch the 'reserved' sign from a neighbouring table and place it on your own. The waitress will assume you are a regular customer, favoured by the boss.

Or there's the popular Lingo Technique based on the premise that waiters give star treatment only to fellow countrymen. So learn a few words of Italian, French or Chinese greeting. Pronounce from the menu with confidence, if not accuracy.

Indeed, one could go on listing these 'waiter boosters' as they're called. Our files certainly are bursting with them. But for brevity's sake we'll confine them to just a few more:

> Casually mention to a fellow diner, in the waiter's hearing, that you think those spots of hers could be mumps. They'll naturally speed the order to ease you both back into the street as soon as possible.

> Utter a few words of German (at least Germanic-sounding words) or display a copy of Sterne. Waiters believe that all Germans are wealthy and consequently good tippers.

> Fit a brown paper cover over a paperback, ostentatiously marked, 'tipping etiquette'.

> If you fail to catch the waiter's eye to collect the bill, stand up, put on your coat and hat, and reach for your handbag or brolly. Volubly make for the door.

How to Get a Free Table

The first thing you should do to win priority service is to say to the first waiter you see, 'How nice to see you again.' This should be done even if you've never been in the place before. All restaurant staff love a 'regular' customer, yet despite false civilities, they only ever recognize a face if it disappeared last time without paying.

Another thing you should know is that when a restaurateur apologizes for having no tables free this is not what he means at all. You'll notice that this 'information' is followed by, 'Meanwhile, would madam and sir like to have something in our waiting area?'

This small space is better decorated than the rest of the premises and it always looks out on the street. The purpose is twofold: (a) to sell you highly-priced drinks from the bar; and (b) to give the impression to the public who pass the window that the restaurant is amazingly popular and therefore top notch.

If one uses the magic incantation, 'Very kind of you, but I think we may have to go to Luigi's instead,' a table will miraculously come free.

The Silver Screen or How to Beat the Time-Bandits

Cinema-going is the thief of time. Queuing for blockbusters, waiting to buy ice-cream and sitting through those adverts for 'a taste of oriental paradise' which, from a scratchy addition tagged to the end of the film, turns out to be the cramped Chinese take-away plus two tables next to the chip shop, is all a bit much. Sensible time-savers wait for films to appear on TV instead.

But if you yearn for the wide screen and wrap-around stereo sound, there are ways and means to make the pleasure outweigh the tedium.

Begin with a phone call. Don't ask when the 'full programme' starts, but the actual big film. Staff can be unhelpful here – they *want* you to see the ads and trailers. Tell them you're a hospital consultant, and mustn't be out of contact for too long. NB: A hospital consultant is someone who once gave directions to the local infirmary.

It's also sensible to tie the cinema down to an exact time for the end of the feature. Once this happens you have a contract. There's nothing wrong with a purely verbal agreement: your rights aren't diminished. You pay to see a film ending at a certain time. Should the programme overrun (it nearly always does) and you miss the last bus home, charge the cinema for the cost of a taxi.

Few cinemas have customer car-parks nowadays. Venal proprietors sell them off to build shops. Even so they keep a small number of parking spaces for staff only. What cheek! The tendency should be countermanded by leaving your vehicle there 'by mistake'. A copy of a cinema magazine or a torch placed on the back window-ledge will imply that you work at the cinema anyway.

In fact, parking in all kinds of staff car-parks is general practice among many of my students who resent this clear example of a modern failing: servers are treated better than customers.

No Queues are Good Queues

The cinema world is a place where the worst of the old meets the worst of the new. We've lost the best traditions like double seats on the back row and opportunities to throw orange peel. Yet we still have to wait in rain-soaked, windswept lines for the most popular new films.

We're compelled to suffer this outrage by greedy managers. They hope to imply that the show is so good the whole town wants to see it. Foil them. Stroll along at the last minute, adopting what's known as the Toad-in-the-Hole ploy.

This involves pushing in between numbers six and seven in the queue, while saying to no one in particular, 'Thanks for saving my place.' Number seven believes this arrangement was made with number six before he arrived. Number six still has his place so couldn't care less anyway.

Two simple precautions are advisory. If you pause to tie your shoelace you can quickly sum up whether numbers six and seven know each other. And it's safer if number six doesn't have an infant

The **TOAD**-in-the-**HOLE** ploy:—
Illustrating the folly of failing to heed Precautionary Advice (b)...

(...concerning sabotage potential of small children)

in tow. Children are both observant and outspoken, a combination which Scroogists find disconcerting.

Naturally the Toad-in-the-Hole can be applied to almost any kind of queue.

Another fine addition to our 'Q-Busters', as our Trans-Atlantic Group calls them, relinquishes the need to join a waiting line at all. All you do is confide to the manager that a member of your party, or yourself if alone, is prone to fainting should he have to stand for too long. This, you tell him, could be followed by foaming at the mouth, which, though not dangerous, has been known to cause panic. All your party will quickly be escorted inside.

The Sammy Explained

My cousin Tony, of whom you'll hear quite a lot in this volume, has some success with a mid-range Q-Buster which he calls the Sammy (not even he knows why). This is only possible at multi-screen cinemas. It involves the assumption of a grim and crusty expression which is worn to request an interview with the manager.

In view of your forbidding mien she'll be expecting a complaint. Instead you say something like, 'I've just seen *The Revenge of the Blood Beast* in your Screen Six and I'm so impressed with the amazing quality of *that* sound I'm now going to see whatever is on at Screen One.'

The manager will be so flattered, and at the same time relieved that you weren't complaining about the tiny size of the screen, that he'll pop into the box office to buy your tickets for you. Or, if you're lucky, escort you into Screen One at no charge. Needless to say you never were in Screen Six at all.

Though allow me to add two notes about the Sammy. Firstly, it is a typical example of Rainman's Reversal, i.e. by appearing to be about to say something nasty, only to come out with something pleasant after all, you can promote in your opponent a feeling of magnanimity towards you, based on relief.

My second aside about the Sammy is not a reflection on its general effectiveness, but more of an amusing story. When I experimented with it at the Bijou in Doncaster, I was thwarted by the manager who said not a word to my comments about sound, but instead cheerfully waved the Blackburn edition of *SuperScrooge* in my face.

In Loo of the Cinema

While the show is under way the optimum time to visit the toilet is straight after a hectic piece of action, a shock or an emotional drama. This is because screen writers have learned cynically to space out the good bits with a stopwatch. In modern films the entertainment value ebbs and flows regularly, like tides on a beach.

The Ice-cream War

One reason why ice-cream vendors in cinemas are always adorned by a long queue is that they never have change. So when someone at the front hands over a five-pound note stride cheerfully from the back with a wealth of silver. Solve the problem and you'll be in a prime position to be served next.

Theatrical Disasters – Avoidance Techniques

What about those theatre productions which are a criminal waste of time? The trouble is that having parted with an enormous fee to see impoverished rubbish, people numb the pain by deluding themselves into thinking they enjoyed it.

They strain out guffaws at unfunny jokes. They clap to melodies which aren't there. Afterwards they tell friends about their 'really good night out'. And with what result? More hapless punters fritter away yet more time patronizing theatrical tripe. It might, as a consequence, run for years.

The only way to see *worthwhile* musicals, plays and reviews is to read full criticisms by a journalist you respect. Then take a second opinion from another one.

Whatever you do, take no notice of one-liners like 'I laughed . . . till I was sick . . .' which appear outside the theatre and in newspaper advertisements. What the reviewer probably wrote was, 'I laughed (not once) till I was sick (with boredom).'

If you do find yourself at a duff performance, don't waste your evening grumpily seeing it through. Confront the manager with the Goods and Services Act. This requires her to sell only that which is fit for the purpose it was intended, i.e. to entertain. Tell her you weren't. A judge would probably throw the case out, but will the manager know this?

You can make your stand more impressive by:

(a) Mentioning your 'legal experience'. You once watched Rumpole of the Bailey, didn't you?

(b) Making your scene in front of people queuing for the next performance.

Practising at the Bar

Getting to the theatre bar first at the interval is a problem which can be solved by buying your gin and tonic before curtain up. Then set it to the side of the counter and ask the barman to stand guard through the first half.

A friend of mine likes to go one better by putting one of her 'temporarily closed' notices on the bar doors just before the performance begins. Not really fair, is it? Pretty clever, though.

If an ice-cream seller appears in front of the stage, you can save energy by foisting your order onto a stranger sitting in the next seat who's about to buy from her. Cloak this request in the language of responsible concern by adding, 'There's no sense in disturbing those around us with *two* trips is there?'

When leaving a theatre don't forget the side entrances. They avoid negotiating log jams in the foyer, and will get you away first in the only available taxi.

Because there is no other door, putting this notice up will allow an extra 17 seconds to reach the theatre bar first.

The Great Outdoor Concert – Moving to the Front

Unless you have telescopic eyes the only conventional way to secure a reasonable view of an outdoor concert is to be the Prime Minister or Princess Diana. Otherwise, simply to see the performers' faces you will need to waste most of the day by arriving very early – an unthinkable prospect for a SuperScrooge.

Pavarotti Play or Golden Curls

It's hard to know just how many of our modest movement were at the 1991 Pavarotti concert in Hyde Park. But as it was free, they must have numbered many thousands. Anyway there's no doubt that the following SuperScrooge strategy was named the Pavarotti Play after that fine artistic spectacle.

The object of PP is to move from the back of the crowd to the front, without pushing. All you need is a rather panicky manner and a distraught expression. Keep asking plaintively, 'Has anyone seen a little girl with a yellow dress and blonde curls?' as you move forward through the crowd.

Trials at a huge pop concert in Wembley prove that it can take as little as seven minutes to progress thirty yards with Pavarotti Play. Even though little can be heard at this sort of show, the silent attitude of 'distraught parent looking for infant in danger' is easily noticed.

At a few outside performances Scroogists at the intermediate level have been able to move as much as twenty-seven yards in only four minutes by adding tearfully, '. . . and she's only five!'

Other Examples of Crowd Control

Cousin Barney, always one for a drama, evolved an even simpler method of slicing through a standing audience. 'Make way, please, I'm a doctor', he would cry in urgent tones. It was always wrongly assumed that someone had collapsed at the front and he was anxious to save a life.

Variation

A rarer form of crowd-easement is to carry a sheaf of old newspapers. The massed audience will always part to make way for that familiar figure – the seller of souvenir issues.

Disguising yourself as a security guard is not on. But is is accepted that you don't have to contradict those who *assume* you are an official. You may perhaps be wearing a T-shirt printed with 'Bloggs Security' on the front. This is a prudent investment as it can be re-used *ad infinitum*.

But don't be tempted to pretend a disability in the hope that you'll be allowed to move to the front of an outdoor audience. Some who've tried this have found themselves whisked off into first aid vans by St John Ambulance members anxious to justify their free tickets.

Exodus

The way to leave an outdoor concert is to time it so that you slink off halfway through the last song. Remember there is always an encore. Very few fans will want to miss even one note from their idol, but for the sake of sacrificing a few choruses you can avoid the crushing exodus. You'll arrive home two hours earlier than everybody else.

In the Club

Many people waste time by arriving too early for cabaret entertainments. This is because they're terrified of coming late and attracting jibes from the performer of the 'I'm glad you could come' variety. But you might just be able to avoid this embarrassment if you've prepared the odd response to shout back such as:

> Comedian: 'Late again I see.'
> Self: 'You're still up there on the stage then . . . forgotten, but not gone!'

Getting served at your table is always tricky in clubland. Anyone trying to catch the waitress's eye will, of course, be snubbed. Our Sussex group came up with the most basic of many suggested solutions to this problem, but it's probably the best. They recommend staging a noisy row with friends. Waiters, it's thought, will draw near out of sheer nosiness. Then you can suddenly cease the quarrel, and put in your order.

Disco Queues – How to Beat Them

Some of the most fashionable discotheques fill up quickly, especially at the weekend. But you can arrive late and still gain entry by wearing something colourful and eye-catching. Bouncers have instructions to encourage anyone who'll: (a) make the club look fashionable; and (b) liven the place up.

If you're being forced to go to a disco by your partner when you'd rather be at home with cocoa and slippers, arrive in dowdy attire. A woman should wear a cardigan and a man a sports jacket, preferably with one of those pocket watches you anchor in the button hole. However glamorous your partner, you'll still be rejected for lowering the trendy tone. Owners know that just a few unprepossessing customers can ruin a disco for a night and the club's reputation for good.

Leisure

It is impossible to enjoy idling thoroughly unless one has plenty of work to do.

—*Jerome K. Jerome*

IF this book has a primary aim then it's to allow you more hours to do the things you *like* to do, rather than *have* to do. But you can – and this section is dedicated to the concept – even save time on doing the things you like to do, making them even more pleasurable. If you see what I mean.

Take reading. If you finish a good novel twice as quickly, you could read two books in the time available. A time-saving gardener will grow twice as many flowers and vegetables.

Sounds obvious, but most people believe that if they dawdle over their pleasures they enjoy them more. They don't, because the achievement is less.

A second leg to the pursuit of energy conservation (and its transference to others) in the field of personal leisure is that it will turn up opportunities to enhance your image, which may be dowdy, by professing impressive outdoor and indoor pursuits you haven't time to perfect or even pursue.

It would do your social and business standing a power of good if it was believed you were an authority on Shakespeare, a part-time archaeologist, or a licensed air pilot. As this sort of study would take up a valuable slice of life, the conventional investment in theory and practice is out of the question.

But you can give an *impression* of being a Shakespeare *aficionado* or an expert archaeologist by employing a few specially designated Scroogisms.

How to Read Five Times More Quickly

You can gallop through a book or magazine (company report or cornflake packet) by scanning down the middle of the page only. If you soften the focus of your eyes, your brain won't just take in the middle three words on every line – it will see them all.

You don't need to practise this technique, just be confident that you aren't missing anything. You can test your ability by 'central scanning' one page then reading it conventionally to check you did

indeed take it all in. You'll be surprised how easy it is. After all, though I may be censured by MI6 for revealing it, master spies use this method for reading voluminous secret documents by torchlight the secret world over.

The method is much favoured for demonstrating how intelligent you are. I find it particularly useful when shown a heavy report by my employer. I glance through it, and he has back in his hands in moments what might have taken twenty minutes to read himself.

Of course, if your aim is simply to impress, showing off on a train for instance, you can turn over the pages of a novel in quick-fire fashion without actually reading anything at all.

Pretending You've Read a Book when You Haven't

It's more indicative of keen social and business powers, and your general up-to-dateness, to be more familiar with the latest novels and non-fiction than with the classics. There are two ways of appearing to do this, without spending much time.

Read a review of the novel or do what reviewers themselves do and study the fly-leaf. Fly-leaf perusal is perfectly acceptable to proprietors of bookshops, whereas browsing through the text is considered bad form.

The way to convey to others that you've read a certain book, even if you haven't, is never to discuss the plot or contents (very dangerous) but to criticize. Useful praises relevant to most books, good or bad, are:

(a) It took some time to get going.

(b) It lost momentum around the middle.

(c) There wasn't as much substance to her minor characters as one would have expected.

(d) I'm surprised someone of her background didn't elaborate on the broader African perspective.

A convincing comment about a new book you haven't seen is, 'Not at all bad, but where was the same control of her first three novels? It wasn't quite there, was it?' This confirms that you've not only read the author's latest but all the earlier ones too. (If you're uncertain whether the author has written anything else you should say, 'Not quite as good as the earlier ones she wrote under the usual pseudonym.')

Oscar Wilde – A Gambit

Another way of proving one's literary prowess without mistreating time in fruitless study is found in the relatively under-used Oscar Wilde Ploy. Yet the methodology is pure simplicity. All that's involved is learning a few Wildean *bons mots* such as, 'Nothing Succeeds Like Failure.' You tell your admiring audience that Wilde wasn't that great a wit because his reputation was based merely on twisting sentences. This invests you with the reputation as a well-read literary expert.

A related gambit is to play off a literary giant against a mere well-known. Example: 'I sometimes prefer Christopher Marlowe to Shakespeare for the vivid colouration of his dialogue.' Or: 'Occasionally even Dickens comes a poor second to Wilkie Collins with the latter's unsurpassable sense of dark foreboding.'

To avoid anyone discovering your paucity of knowledge, you should, after a suitable length of literary discussion, row into safer waters by saying gaily, 'But we're not going to go on about stuffy old books all night are we, surely? So where are you going on your holidays, Vickie?' This rapid change of tack into a lighter vein will dispel any suspicion that you're an academic show-off, while the raw respect will remain.

How to Spot a Book Which May Be a Waste of Time

Few novels, even badly written ones, can be universally dismissed as time-wasters. One reader's 'can't-put-it-down' is another's 'load-of-old-rubbish'. But a lot of non-fiction, particularly self-help guides, are exercises in waffle around one or two jaded ideas and aren't worth the reading.

But how *do* you choose, given the limited opportunities to assess content in the bookshop?

Tomlinson, buyer for the SuperScrooge Library in Gray's Inn Road, has given us permission to present his personal guide to this conundrum. When considering a 'How-to book' as they're called, pick one page towards the middle and count up how many things you didn't know about the subject. If it's less than 12 put it down again.

Also beware of works with a surfeit of blank pages, wide margins, large print, abnormal gaps between lines and chapter headings which take up the whole page. Personally I never buy a volume which has more than eight pages before the introduction.

A Night Away from the Opera

Nothing builds a business and social reputation more than a crammed schedule of visits to the opera, ballet and theatre. Ah, the glamour, the glitter, the intellectual stimulation, the unbounded adulation accorded to a dedicated patron of the arts . . . If *only* we had time, because naturally, all we really want to do after a hard day is to slump in front of the telly.

It's clear the sensible course is to lead others to think we were in the royal box when we weren't. Not easy, you might think, and indeed not. But our Mayfair Section have not let us down and their suggestions follow:

Indicating how to get the optimum number in a royal box.

(a) Leave a sealed envelope on your desk marked, 'from the Hippodrome', or place the evening paper there, with the theatre advert circled in red.

(b) Say loudly on the phone, 'Ah, you recognized my voice ... good ... our usual seats I think ... ah you remembered, Thomas ... the dress circle. ...' Then quote your credit card number.

(c) Read the new reviews so you can comment on the production next day.

(d) Don't say anything, but change into your evening dress at work before going home.

And now a superior way of cementing your reputation as a patron of the performing arts, The Celebrity Call-Back. Like all the best ploys it requires both planning and skilful timing. Ring up the theatre during a matinée and ask to speak to a well-known member of the cast. As he'll be on stage he'll have to call you back.

Leave only your first name and number. Suggest a time. Make sure you're out then but that someone at work can take a message. As the star may well know someone with your first name, he'll doubtless return the call, asking for you. He'll supply his famous name and ask *you* to ring back.

Naturally, it will soon get round the office that you're so much of a theatre buff that you're actually on first-name terms with the stars.

Should the Celebrity Call-Back slightly misfire and you do find yourself speaking to a theatrical personality, it's best to admit all. They'll be flattered. The much-loved Jimmy Edwards, comedian and headmaster of the admirable Chiselbury School, once treated me to an expensive meal after I'd unwittingly enrolled him in my little scheme.

The Fast Way to See Museums and Exhibitions

Does anyone really want to shuffle round museums and art galleries? Yet we all feel guilty if we don't, especially when at large in a historic city like London or York. So how can we comfortably shorten the visit to concentrate on more rewarding pastimes including, perhaps, the first-hand study of architectural styles in older taverns?

The first essential is to arrive just twenty minutes before closing time. Explain to the rest of your party that this is when there'll be fewer people around so you can all have a better view.

Museum visiting requires its own kind of breathless enthusiasm to dissuade any of your group from sitting down. Research from Catterick shows that museum-trudging is three times more exhausting than housework and, without rest, your party will soon want to pack it in.

A peerless time-saver, guaranteed to lustre your reputation as an art connoisseur, is to say, 'Leave the Turners and Constables. They're a bit chocolate boxy, aren't they. Let's go straight to the Blinkington-Smyths.' You can cut out most of the pictures this way.

If anybody dithers over the Egyptian mummies, casually mention that you've read how some deadly germs can lie dormant for thousands of years.

I also carry an empty camera on these occasions. The trick here is to point it at a famous picture and wait for an angry attendant to usher you all out of the room, if not the building. Waving an umbrella point near the canvas has the same effect.

How to 'Holiday Abroad' Without Wasting Two Weeks

While open, as always, to correction I have this feeling that no accomplished Scroogist ever really yearns for a yearly four-week sojourn in tropical sunshine (two weeks in sub-tropical sun impresses no one, by the way). Who, it's argued, needs any kind of relaxing break when the arts of getting someone else to do all the work have been thoroughly mastered?

Yet you must still supply signs that an expensive, exotic holiday has been taken or suffer the set-back to your high-living reputation by gossipers who'll say you can't afford it.

With a little forethought you can buttonhole any colleagues going to Malaya, Jamaica, Sri Lanka, Borneo or China (never Spain, France, Italy, Greece or Turkey) and ask them to bring back some postcards 'for your collection'.

In one or two years' time you can write on these picture-cards some vague nonsense on traditional themes, such as 'the weather's marvellous' and 'wish you were here'. Then squeeze in at the bottom, in a different coloured ink, 'Sorry about delay. Postal strike in Borneo. Had to mail in Britain.'

Perfectionists will want to enlarge on this ploy by sending all the cards in a packet to a post office near Heathrow or Gatwick. An accompanying note should implore the postmaster to forward the stamped enclosures with the rest of his mail.

There's absolutely no need, however, to go to the lengths of obtaining an artificial bronzing in the high street. A deep tan is regarded as tacky nowadays, and you can always explain your pallidness with the proven standbys, 'Who wants to waste time cooking on sand with all those archeological wonders to explore?' or, 'You can't dance the night away and get up in the mornings as well.'

Single people can then add conspiratorily, ' . . . and who wants to?', thus suggesting that their 'exotic holiday' produced the lover of their dreams.

Zoo Time – How to Save it

Many zoological managements give residence to a few genuinely interesting animals, like polar bears and gorillas, and to a lot more commonplace creatures like squirrels, rats, pigs and grass snakes, only to make up the numbers.

You can save some time by studying the zoo plan to avoid the rodent house, the aviary, the aquarium and the insect house whose denizens are usually hiding under stones.

Actually the quickest way to see animals in captivity (as explained in *SuperScrooge*) is to prowl the perimeter looking at the taller animals who poke over the walls.

But if you're forced to pay for entry by the entreaties of a young family, and you still want to leave early, you won't do better than the 'Can Stand It No Longer' technique. This involves peering at a tigress or panther forever stalking a tiny cage, throwing up your hands in horror at the cruelty of it all and hurrying from the zoo, no doubt followed by your now sympathetic children.

Tips for the Races

There are still a select few who make such a handsome living out of betting on horses that some bookmakers have gone so far as to ban them from laying a bet. While interviewing some of these top punters for a radio programme, they told me as one voice that the only secret is to minutely study form day after day.

As this edition's uppermost aim is to circumvent such dedication, I can now reveal a way to pick a winning horse without knowing its antecedence at all. It makes the form book redundant, yet as far as I know it's a system no other racing expert has divulged (in print) before.

Simply buy a ticket for the paddock and study the entrants as they parade around. Or rather examine what they produce. For it's my experience that horses which appear to have diarrhoea do very well indeed.

Though no one in the veterinary profession has recorded an official reason why this might be, it's not hard to guess a probable link with the dramatically speeded-up actions of a human when he's in a hurry to go in a hurry.

How to Put a Bet On Quickly

A wise backer waits till the last minute to strike his wager on the course. That's because the odds vary for each bookie depending on how much he's taken on your horse. The trouble is that by this time a small crowd is often clamouring for their bets to be taken just before the off. The way to get your last-minute wager on before this lot is to shout, 'Big money bet . . . big money bet!' Your money will then be taken at once.

The fact that you've handed over only £1 might evince a bad-natured comment from the bookmaker that this isn't a big bet. If you bother to reply it should be, 'It might not be a lot of money to you, sir, but to someone without a job, a repossessed home and five children. . . .'

How to Win Indoor Games

One of the pastimes most satisfying to the Scroogist is the boxed game, like Monopoly or Careers. It's best for one person to read the rules in advance so that time isn't lost by constant reference to the instruction booklet as the game proceeds. You can also win much quicker by being this person and secretly adapting the rules to your advantage.

It's easy to succeed in an armchair quiz contest like Trivial Pursuits by stacking the cards after looking up a few answers pre-game.

One can also shorten a traditional game like draughts by removing the front row of pieces. A rapid chess match can be started without pawns. Hopefully your opponent won't realize it, but you need a completely different set of strategies and skills to play a curtailed game. If you practise a few moves beforehand you can wipe the board with an opponent who would normally walk all over you in a conventional match.

'It's not the winning of the game that counts – it's winning it quickly' (Blenkinson).

Home Is Where the Clock Is

Home of lost causes and forsaken beliefs and unpopular names
and impossible loyalties.

—*Matthew Arnold, 1822–1888*

JUST like accidents, most time-wasting occurs in the home (with
the one exception of solicitors' offices). This is because we are more
relaxed *chez nous*. Time doesn't seem as pressing as it does at work or
when living it up on the town.

We feel we have more precious moments to give away, to our
partners, children and visitors. We're happy to labour long and hard
on trivial tasks, because we're working for ourselves, our own
family. Yet because so many hours are frittered away in domestics,
it's probably worth giving the underlying causes that much more
attention.

We begin with a basic – shifting the work onto other members of
the household.

Exploiting that Guilty Feeling

An all-purpose rule for transferring unpleasant chores onto others is
to make members of the family feel guilty about not working as hard
as they should. This is done by Subliminal Trivialization – in other
words faintly ridiculing the task they're doing at the moment.

Imagine your husband is mowing the lawn. You're reading the
paper. But dirty pots are in the sink. The approved thing to do is
walk outside and demand, 'Will you be *long* doing that?' The fine
accusing tone here, with stress on the word 'long', suggests that he is
idling his time away and needs to purge this sin in some way. The
way is now clear for you to re-appear after a few minutes and
request, 'Would you mind doing the washing up then? When you've
got a moment, of course.' This time, place the main emphasis on
'when' with a minor stress on 'of course'.

The earlier question, 'will you be long?', has a secondary use. It
implies your husband is dawdling over his lawn-cutting and needs
to speed up.

With a few small adjustments this text-book example of Trivialization can be employed over and over again, not just in a domestic
setting, but in most other arenas too.

Exploiting that Guilty Feeling – the Fiona Variation

My sister Fiona pleaded that her Feeling Guilty gambit should not be exposed here as my dim brother-in-law Derek will discover a dodge which has worked against him for 11 years now. But its important contribution to our science compels me so to do.

She's perfected a way of making Derek not only do many chores, but to adopt them as regular duties. A beautiful example of her art was staged in the conservatory.

Fiona had always watered the plants. She was doing so on the day she suddenly announced, 'My bougainvillea has died.' Such was her mastery of the declamatory tone, her stress on the word 'died', that Derek was made to feel this was his fault in some way, that he'd been remiss in an unspoken promise to care for everything she holds dear. Struck with an ill-defined feeling of remorse he's been doing Fiona's watering ever since.

You recognize the flexibility of the technique? It can also be brought to bear in the garden, for pet care, looking after children, any situation where anything living is in some kind of peril, usually quite imaginary. . . .

How to Just Pop Out for a Minute

It's hard to over-stress the importance of this skill, which like trivialization, helps you have an enjoyable time, while someone else tackles chores normally down to you.

Here's a common example, simplified for this popular exposition, of this advanced Scroogist theory. Your partner is polishing the silver. You say, 'I'm just going to town to pay the paper bill and take the library books back.' So far the trip sounds like a jolly jaunt. But it can be made to sound more arduous and time-consuming by adding, 'I'll probably do a few other things while I'm there. We need some potatoes, don't we?'

Your wife is quite content with the suggestion as she's now planning to stop for a covert cup of tea while you're away.

While donning your coat, inquire, 'Could you plant those daffodil bulbs while I'm out?' Potter about a bit more before adding, 'Oh, and I was going to clean the toilet.'

Then pass through the front door only to return with the afterthought, 'and I'd intended to sweep the front path if I could find the time.'

By this time you've gradually built up quite a hefty extra schedule for your wife without her actually realizing it. You can now go to the pub for a couple of hours, pick up a few spuds on the way home and complain bitterly that both the newsagents and the library were shut.

Getting Rid of Unwanted Callers

Though we usually resent them, there are still niceties to be observed in dealing with professional time-wasters who invade our sanctum like they've never done before. It's easy, of course, to slam doors in local politicians' faces and bring down phones on salesmen. But there's no skill, or indeed fun, in solving any problem of time conservation by being rude.

(Fairly Straight) Ways to Get Rid of Unwanted Callers

If a *brush salesgirl* calls, buy something small. Nothing works faster to see her off. And it saves time getting the same article from a shop later on.

Religious cultists persist in persisting even if you should keel over on the doorstep. The *only* way to dispel them is to claim you're a prominent member of an orthodox religion.

Local councillors and other electioneers won't waste breath preaching to the converted. Promise to support their party on polling day, even if you don't.

Fitted kitchen salesmen can be informed you had new units fitted just last week.

Double-glazing salesmen should be told you've been made bankrupt.

More Advanced Ways to Tackle Unwanted Callers

Put on your overcoat before answering the front door. It will seem you're on your way out.

Place a magazine picture of a pit-bull terrier in the window. Ram home the advantage by dripping spots of rust paint on the front step.

Walk heavily to the front door. Pause a few seconds, with nose pressed against the glass. Walk away without opening up. The caller will think you are deranged.

Upstage a doorstep salesman by trying to sell him your kettle. Be quite insistent.

Open the door waving a whisky bottle. Sway dangerously and babble. An incoherent Celtish-sounding mock dialect is best, as it suggests violence.

The deterrent effect of ploy two can be enhanced by stuffing a pair of old slacks with newspaper, popping slippers on the extremities

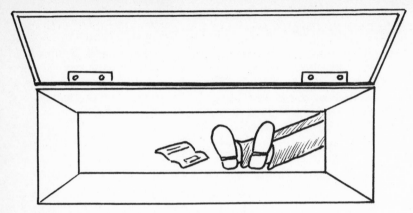

More advanced ways to tackle unwanted callers.

and poking what appears to be a murdered body from the living room into the hall. Callers who peer through the letterbox will be shocked into hasty departure.

The more permanent way to deal with callers you don't want is to site the doorbell eighteen inches from the ground, perhaps obscured by a curl of ivy. Divulge the secret location only to visitors you like – and to enemies with back trouble.

How to Deal with Telephone Sellers

Should someone ring up and offer double-glazing, it's no good pretending you can't hear them on a defective phone. They'll only try again. Instead say in hushed tones that you can't talk now as there's been a death in the family. No need to explain that your goldfish died four years ago.

Another remedy is to reply to the caller in a mock Slavonic language (this sounds like recorded speech played backwards). Warning: Never try a few phrases of a language you vaguely know. You'll find, embarrassingly, that a good few foreign students become part-time telephone salesmen to supplement their incomes.

Ending Unwanted Social Telephone Calls

A reliable indicator that a SuperScrooge is in residence is the small piece of cellophane paper kept by the phone. Then if a friend shows no sign of freeing the line as your favourite TV programme approaches, you can gently crackle the paper close to the mouthpiece. This will sound like your home is burning down. All you need to do is shout, 'Good Heavens, I've left the chip pan on!' and hurriedly ring off.

An even simpler way of terminating interminable calls is to rap on the telephone table. Announce that the doctor or the vicar is without. I'm not sure why a call from either of these professionals should silence telephone bores, but it does. Perhaps they subconsciously link such visitors with death.

Some serious time-savers use a battery-powered doorbell mounted on a wooden square for long-winded callers. They say this is more convincing than the knuckle rap, but I'm not so sure.

Actually, there's no real need to answer the phone in the first place. Any urgent call will always be repeated in less than five minutes . . . whether it's a road accident or a win on the pools.

How to Keep Your Own Telephone Calls Short

Supposing you have to make a duty call to an aged aunt or uncle. You're worried about your status in their will, but you really need to get some serious drinking done. The standard gambit here is to whisper hoarsely and complain about your sore throat. You're afraid you'll lose your voice completely if you keep talking much longer.

When the telephone or doorbell rings exploit the curiosity of others in your household by kindly allowing them to be the first to answer. This saves many hours a year.

Everybody Needs Neighbours – as Mugs

How often have you fretted around the home waiting in vain for plumbers, repairers and delivery men. Yet this inconvenience can be avoided by putting the onus on a neighbour. Leave the keys with the old dear or the young couple next door and ask them to let your visitor in. The advantages of this third-party approach far outweigh the infinitesimal chance of your neighbour having previous convictions.

To begin with, the woman next door, weighed down with the responsibility of it all, will keep a sharper ear open for your caller. So he won't find it quite so easy to brush the knocker ever so lightly then leave a note regretting you weren't in, before scampering away to an early finish.

The work will be better supervised too, as the neighbour will now be petrified that the tradesperson might pocket the silver, for which she might have to answer.

Neighbours are also good for bringing washing in, feeding cats, baby-sitting, dog-sitting, holding stakes for pools collectors, passing on their magazines and newspapers and many other bountiful tasks.

Domestic scientists everywhere agree that the chap next door will happily carry out all sorts of favours in exchange for the flattery of being entrusted with keys. All you need do is ask. And the beauty of it is that you won't need to return any similar services because they'll never quite trust you with their keys.

Especially if you take the precaution of looking slightly shifty whenever you meet. (The rapid side-to-side eye movement should be practised quite carefully so that it lasts only a second. Any longer looks stagey.)

People are more willing – and did we really need all that research by the sociology department of Edlington University to tell us this – to help neighbours of advancing years than they are younger ones. So if you are getting on, there's merit in exaggerating the fact when you meet, or believe you are being observed by, the folk next door.

Walk hesitatingly with a stoop, clutch hold of gate posts. Struggle arthritically with the dustbin lid. Drop it as your fingers fail to grasp. Consolidate the impression by contorting your face with effort as you painfully mount the front steps. Offers to do the shopping and the gardening will come flooding in.

My Uncle Dennis heightens this gambit by cheerfully regretting that his younger relatives never visit him any more. He also asks neighbours, 'Not bad is it for 84?', even though he's only 63. Like all in this happy fraternity of modern-day Scrooges he's proud that this doesn't involve telling a lie, arguing privately that he never actually said he was 84.

The younger person's version of the above is to acquire one of those telescopic light-weight crutches for moving painfully around the back garden and up and down the street. But note that the professional approach here is *not* to limp. Using such an aid while not hobbling gives the impression that you have a serious complaint infinitely more worthy of practical help than a mere twisted ankle or broken leg.

House Guests who Come to Stay . . . and Stay . . . and Stay

It's hard to shift relatives who outstay their welcome. By definition they'll be pretty thick-skinned. You can try rubbing the dog's jaws with bicarbonate of soda to stimulate the later symptoms of rabies, but people can be pretty unobservant.

And though they're not likely to miss the time-honoured convention of making ghostly sounds at 2 a.m., this old favourite is now in recession following over-exposure in sitcoms on ITV.

Still worth a try though is a routine known as the 'Plate-catcher', *viz*, when you feel you've had quite enough of your guest, stage a series of rows with a permanent member of the family. Let these altercations grow in intensity. Grossly embarrassed at having to keep the peace every night the visitor will soon pack her bags and leave you to it.

How my brother Richard once succeeded in solving the unwanted house-guest problem is more than worth a mention. Stuck with our Aunt Mary week after week, he finally indicated with a tick in red ink some ghastly contagion in his medical dictionary. The clause 'some-times fatal' was underlined. This page was left open on the kitchen table. Then he took to bed 'under strict doctor's orders' not to breathe

When all else fails — The PLATE-CATCHER routine can be employed to speed the parting guest — HIGHLY effective, but expensive and exhausting

near anyone. Faced with the double peril of doing all the work and risking infection, Aunt Mary packed and disappeared shortly after tea.

Richard will never know if his extra precaution of removing a small but important condenser from the TV set also encouraged the exodus. In any event, Aunt Mary could be said to have had the last laugh, because this part was never seen again.

Cleaning Up With the Cleaner

Every household needs a cleaning lady or gentleman once a week. As well as eliminating drudgery, it allows you to impress by casually referring to 'my domestic staff' at parties.

We've all met people who take the mistaken moral view that this is not quite right as we should all be prepared to clear up our own muck. How misguided! This attitude is to disparage the pride most of these skilful practitioners have in keeping homes spotless in a third of the time. (It's the last five words which count.)

An annual Christmas present and a holiday postcard will soon strengthen the relationship to the point where you can ask your cleaner to take your washing home, iron it, fold it, mind the baby/dog/cat and shop when you break, or appear to break, your ankle. In fact, the more you make her a trusted member of the family, the more she'll be content to do the family's donkey work.

If you do find your cleaner isn't performing to standard, don't admonish her. This could imperil the family retainer relationship. Merely engage her in general gossip while absent-mindedly drawing your finger across an ornament to glance fleetingly at the resultant dust.

You may also find it prudent to arrange your day-off to coincide with her visit to stop her sliding off early which she will do in your absence.

An important factor in keeping a domestic up to scratch is to invest her with an instant reputation she'll feel obliged to live up to. This is the type of line to use: 'My cousin Gillian has a cleaner, too. But she's not a patch on you, Mary. Not a patch . . .' As you say this hold up a brass poker or some such and admire it. Experiencing a sudden surge of pride, she'll give your home more attention from now on. (Some authorities say twice as much.)

Do-it-Yourself Housework

If you can't get help, don't despair. Our records include hundreds of labour-saving techniques for the home.

> The traditional ploy of sweeping dust under carpets is now out by the way (discovery is all too easy). But disposing of it down cracks in the floorboards is still on our approved list.

> Buy patterned carpets which need vacuuming three times less than plain pale carpets and four times less than plain dark carpets.

> Don't vacuum under rugs or furniture. Never dust the tops of pictures.

> If you slide out of bed carefully you won't need to make it.

> Spray a few drops of silicone polish into the air. This implies you've polished everything in the room.

May I also include the latest entry on this particular file, only recently entered by our domestic team. If you leave the washing-machine on, empty, but with some fragrant washing-liquid in the reservoir, an aroma suggesting the house is buzzing with cleaning activity will pervade the air. The steady drone of the machine also contributes to this illusion which is indispensable towards impressing visiting maiden aunts who (and I hope I'm not thought to be obsessed by this theme) may have money to leave.

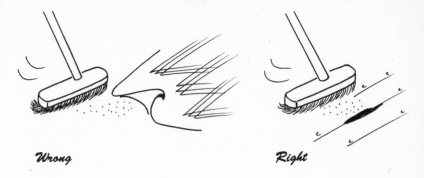

Wrong   *Right*

All Washed Up

The average person spends six months of their life washing-up, according to *Howitt's Domestic Timetable*. Now here's how to cut washing-up drudgery by half.

Wait until you have enough crockery to make it worthwhile, but soak every item as you use it in a bowl of cold water spiced with washing-up liquid.

Fill pans to the top with water, not half-way up as most people do. But don't add cold water to a hot pan. That helps to solder the food on.

Cut down the load. Many vegetables should be cooked in the same pan. If you're in a hurry cold foods, like rice-pudding and fruit can be eaten from the tin. Hot foods can be scoffed from the pan. (I'm too refined to do this myself.)

Omelette pans shouldn't be washed. Wipe around with kitchen roll.

Leave crockery to dry itself, but rinse first. Fellow Europeans can't get over how we put up with detergent-flavoured food.

The Art of Getting Someone Else to Wash-Up – All the Time

All the tips above are wasted on a master of time and energy conservation. Take my cousin Tony. He scorns such direction because someone else in his household always does the washing-up.

Many years ago now he proved his unsuitability to the task by 'accidentally' dropping a few inexpensive cups and saucers. The climax came when he appeared shamefacedly from the kitchen holding two halves of a Royal Worcester jug. It was long after he was banned from the kitchen sink that Aunt Mary realized that the family never owned such a jug.

I later managed to wring from Tony that he actually brought home the pieces from a dustbin outside a local gift shop. This fine strategy should be emulated.

I also favour (but not as much) the allergy method of washing-up avoidance. This involves soaking your hands in cold water, then hanging them out of the window until chapped. The subject can then claim a painful and permanent sensitivity not only to washing-up liquids, but to many other household cleaners.

How to Avoid Pulling Your Weight

Never underestimate the power of impression – in this context the ability to suggest you're achieving a lot of work around the house by doing just a little.

A quintessential example in practice is the folding of washing. Say, for example, that you're faced with an unsorted pile of towels taken from the line. Simply fold two and leave the rest. It's a philosophical conundrum which has puzzled behaviourists through the centuries that, by some peculiar psychological progression, the sight of two folded towels suggests the whole.

The same with ironing, just press the odd skirt or pair of slacks and it curiously appears that you've done the lot.

The Barely-Done Syndrome, as it used to be known, has many facets but it comes into its own in the kind of situation where your partner has entrusted you with the housework while she goes out. On return the appearance of a few hardly-started little jobs make it appear you've been working like a Trojan. In reality you watched TV.

Making the Dustman do More Work for You

The reason dustmen are called refuse-collectors nowadays is that they refuse to take so much stuff. Garden waste and any serious rubbish slightly too big for the dustbin isn't allowed.

To get round the first problem, fill black plastic bags with rose prunings, leaves and weeds. Then sprinkle a few old newspapers on top to disguise the contents.

Or you can wait for the collection vehicle to call, leap forwards and put your garden rubbish in yourself. Being council employees, collectors are not used to moving fast enough to stop you.

Large items should be stored until December. This is when every dustman will collect anything up to, and probably including, a decayed elephant for fear of losing the Christmas tip.

Another device (good fun this) is to call the local scout troop and tell them you have something very desirable for their next jumble sale. Later, on calling, they may secretly look down on your old wheelbarrow with no bottom in it, but they're well-brought-up lads and their disappointment won't show.

The Lodger Dodges

Our humble philosophy smiles on lodgers. Sharing the home with one or more paying guests offers limitless opportunities to save time and effort. True, they'll never readily agree to a substantial task like painting your hall, but there are many modest, but useful, favours they will do, without really noticing the imposition. So practise your opportunism. Begin with these basic lodger requests:

> Wait for your tenant to call at the newsagents for a Sunday paper so you can read it together.

> Borrow your tenant's tea and coffee. This is tolerated as long as you're seen to replace it later. He won't see that it's a cheaper brand as you'll be pouring it back in the same caddy or jar.

> Call out, 'Would you mind buying me some milk/tea/rhubarb chunks?' when your tenant goes shopping.

> Ask your tenant to take in your washing if it rains.

> Study your tenant's habits and try to synchronize them with your own. For example when your lodger goes to the launderette, present a bag of your washing for him to do at the same time.

> Give up going to the library and borrow your tenant's books. You'll probably enjoy broadening your usual choice.

More adventurous time-savers will want to try our 'Cuckoo-in-the-Nest' sequence. Here one 'inadvertently' mixes a pair of underpants, a couple of plain shirts and three pairs of socks into a lodger's soiled linen. Almost invariably he'll wash and dry them without noticing these items aren't his, even, amazingly, if he sees them on the line. Your items can be surreptitiously reclaimed later.

Yet another ploy is to feign illness and retire to your bed. You will be brought soup, toast and reviving cups of tea for about two days before the usual lodger's compassion fatigue sets in. The minute you're abandoned, you can get up.

A minor, but useful, variation on this theme is to claim to have twisted your ankle. This usually encourages lodgers to carry out a few small errands on your behalf.

You can also conserve valuable time normally spent going out to meet people if you hi-jack your lodger's more interesting friends.

And don't overlook that, although the degree of resistance might be somewhat heightened, most of the above labour-saving devices can also be tested on members of the family.

Dating and Marriage

His designs are strictly honourable, as the saying is; that is to rob a
lady of her fortune by way of marriage.

—Henry Fielding's 'Tom Jones'

WE must point out that finding the right man or woman to join
you on the vulnerable passage through life can expend huge
amounts of time, money and effort. So SuperScrooge would be
failing in his duty if he didn't highlight some of the more important
precepts of time-saving in this difficult field.

The overriding principle is not simply to choose the right mate
with a minimum of fuss or bother. You need also to settle with
someone who can save you all the effort you might need to expend
by staying single. That person must therefore be: (a) industrious; and
(b) well-off. (Tolerance is also desirable, but not at the expense of the
two primary requirements.)

This chapter will show you how to recognize that individual and
complete the minimum amount of wooing in the fastest possible
time.

Where to Meet

There are those who say (including Professor Taylor, surprisingly)
that you should avoid entanglements with a colleague at work. How
wrong! All you have to do to discover their financial status or,
equally important, that of their parents, is to tune into office gossip.
You may even have access to personal files to check on salaries.
You'll be able to observe daily just how practically suitable (hard-
working) they are.

Whereas if you date a stranger you'll have to spend at least one
evening trying to discover this information. And then it will be
coloured by their own biased views of themselves.

Another benefit of working relationships [sic] is that you won't
have to travel somewhere to collect your lover to go out every
evening. You can meet up in reception. And there's always that
ready-made subject for serious discourse, office gossip.

But what happens, my critics often ask, when the relationship
founders? Is it not very embarrassing to see your ex-lover every
working day? Well, yes indeed. Which is why you can ask your

employer to transfer you to a different department. And many's the love-crossed star employee who's won early promotion this way.

You May See a Stranger

But not every office is stuffed with attractive propositions. And if you prefer to take chances with a stranger you can avoid finding out too late that they're skint by choosing an affluent location. Put at its crudest this means accepting an invitation to dance at a May Ball and not an inner city disco.

Some of my female students have struck gold in the very best enclosures at fashionable race-meetings. A ploy of the first water here is to affect to lose a winning betting-slip at the feet of a dishy racehorse owner. As every course is littered with hundreds of losing tickets this can take some time. A small sign of distress, a dab of saliva on one cheek (never two), is obviously gainful here.

The Travel Option

Another safe place to start a conversation is in transit. It's worth visiting an airport lounge occasionally because only the wealthy normally travel this way. But check luggage labels to sort the jet-setters from the two-weeks-in-Benidorm types.

My cousin Tony, who's a womaniser and therefore prone to extremes, resorts to the V-shaped tan on these occasions. He daubs his pasty chest with honey-bronze make-up but, to save time and expense, only in the triangular patch revealed by his top three shirt buttons. Though he rarely leaves Leeds, where he's a freelance road-gritter, women on the sharp end of his disarming expertise come to believe he's either a transworld businessman or a well-heeled playboy.

By the same token, the first-class section of trains is another good location. A bus station is a bad one.

Other Favourite Venues

The ordinary house party is a natural pick-up point because one's expected to open every conversation here with the asset-ascertaining questions, 'What do you do?' and 'Where do you live?' (Later in this chapter we deal with the crucial matter of party timing.)

Self-help articles in magazines often advise partner-seekers to adopt the 'join-a-local-association-you'll-find-a-list-of-suitable-ones-at-your-local-library' technique. The advice is only sound if you pick your group with care. This is a vast subject and can only be skated over in a general work. But a few magnets for wealthy members are the Junior Chamber of Commerce, NSPCC supporters, Civic Trust, Lions, Rotarians and clubs for horse enthusiasts.

At the risk of offending, I would be chary of joining an amateur dramatics group, canal restoration societies, sporting clubs in general and an angling association in particular. (Was it the 1948 Winchester Survey which confirmed that people who go fishing tend to be lazy and inattentive lovers?)

Contrary to popular belief political groupings aren't a reliable indicator. Take my childhood sweetheart, Vivien. Having failed to discover a rich suitor at the Conservative Association within a six-month self-imposed deadline, she moved on to join the Labour Party where she met and married a top defence barrister ('top' is her adjective).

The Opening Move (A Philosophical Note)

If you've done your research, you'll not only know that there's money about, with perhaps a parental villa or a yacht in the background, but that your target is both capable and diligent, perhaps skilled in cooking, DIY, gardening and car mechanics.

But how to set about sparking reciprocal interest? The following lessons are suited, in a modern world, to both sexes.

There is absolutely no point in delaying your approach for fear of rejection. If you are spurned it will happen whenever you make your move. And once snubbed, you must give up the quest. To try to protect your investment by trying again and again is to hurl good time after bad. If there's no spark, there'll never be fire.

The Opening Move (In Practice)

The most efficient opener of all is, 'Would you like to go for a drink sometime this week?' Yet the simplicity of this sentence masks a few complexities. The question must be asked on a Monday, and not, say, a Thursday, so the target has six days to choose from and not three. Thus chances of acceptance are doubled.

Never specify an exact day. If you ask, 'Would you like to go for a drink on Tuesday?', there's an opportunity for the reply, 'Sorry, I'm going to my granny's on Tuesday.' You're then forced into the humiliating position of asking about Wednesday, then Thursday, then Friday and so on till you have to say lamely, 'Some other time then.'

The invitation should also come out of the blue. There must be no preliminary small-talk. Once trivial conversation is under way it makes your question harder to raise. A direct approach is also more potent because it enshrines an element of flattery. The object of affection will assume that: (a) your approach is important to you; and (b) you've been plucking up courage for weeks.

These twin beliefs can be enhanced by a certain breathlessness when posing the question. This advantage is obtainable without

(Daddy's rich...)   (Mummy's even richer...)

A - DIY Manual   B - Cordon Bleu Diploma
C - Green fingers   D - Car Maintenance Kit

tell-tale fakery by a medium-fast run up one flight of stairs up to two minutes before the conversation takes place (three minutes for smokers).

When You're Wasting Your Time

One of the greatest services I can do in the ultimate cause of saving time is to set out once again Davidson's Rule of Diminishing Parley. What the great man was able to consolidate after years of patient study (September 1954–May 1990) was that any man or woman being chatted up will unconsciously confirm by how many sentences are uttered whether it is worth the opener's while to persevere.

Should your first line be, 'It's a lovely night, don't you think?' the target may reply, 'Yes, it is. I do love these Lancashire Nights. My mother lived in Macclesfield and she always adored Lancashire nights too.'

This three-sentence reply reveals a strong measure of interest. The final statement even grants what is known among film producers as a 'sequel promiser'. In other words you're left with a clear opportunity to talk about your mother's birthplace.

Should the target get only as far as two sentences, it's worth pursuing the conversation, but you may have to work at it. However, if your only response is a mere 'Yes, it is', or more usually a grunt, then you should give up and move away. Davidson says, and who can doubt him, that it is, and always has been, futile to try to override a snub.

My cousin Tony Parkinson holds, however, that the single sentence snub isn't always the end. He claims that in rare instances changes of mind do occur and the object may voluntarily reopen the proceedings later on. Practically speaking though, the one-sentence riposte marks the end of the game.

The Fastest Way to Attract a Likely Partner at a Party

This, of course, is a matter of timing at its purest. It takes only a few minutes to winkle out the most attractive person present, but it will be some hours before you can proposition. For this reason other experienced love strategists suggest talking to every other guest first, leaving the real object of desire until after midnight.

I disagree. The right procedure is to broach the target early. The moment you've awakened interest (see the chapter on Your Image) disappear into the kitchen to fetch him or her a drink. And don't come back. Then that ancient Aramaic law, You Always Want that which Shoots out of Grasp, or its modern equivalent, the Slippery Soap Theory, swings into play.

All you need do is to re-engage in conversation just before coats are collected and either offer to see the prize home or meet later in the week.

The Importance of Impression on the First Date

Wear jeans and jumper on your first outing and you can probably kiss the target goodbye (and that's not meant literally). Nor should you look too smart. A large floppy hat and a voluminous overcoat are my choice for both sexes. This outfit – common in charity shops – projects an artistic mien, always attractive in a prosaic world.

I'll never forget the insult offered by a female colleague I met in Bond Street whilst wearing my huge black Crombie, once the property of the Chief Constable of Denbighshire, and a large black hat which looked like something John Wayne should have had dry-cleaned but put in the wash.

'Oh, it's you Malcolm, I thought it was somebody interesting', she said, proving the point, but leaving one feeling vaguely upset.

The first outing should not be to a concert, theatre, cinema or night club. Go somewhere where you can chat all evening and so get to know the subject. Otherwise you'll be starting all over again on the next date.

But try to speak as little as you can to establish your credentials as: (a) a sympathetic listener; and (b) a rather mysterious figure. The gambit is also important if you're paying a restaurant bill. The more your partner talks the less will be eaten.

The very best tips on avoiding restaurant charges are listed in all editions of the original SuperScrooge.

HOW TO KEEP A PROMISING RELATIONSHIP ACTIVE

The Personality Incentive

The role of personality in courtship has been a perpetual source of puzzlement for scientific minds all over the globe. Some very respectable research by sociology pioneers in Mexico, Taiwan and Guernsey demonstrates that though most people require their partners to be conventional, staid, grey-suited and incapable of causing embarrassment, this desire only sets in after 11 weeks. Only Senor Morez of Acapulco puts it any higher than $13\frac{1}{4}$ weeks.

Before then, the need is always for an impetuous, outgoing and perhaps even an eccentric romantic figure. This earlier period being crucial to a long-lasting relationship, it follows that a few artificial personality-boosters won't go amiss.

The Personality Incentive (Mysterious)

Even lacklustre positions like teachers or post office clerks have been used as fronts for undercover work of some description. This is the cornerstone of my next machination which conveys the hint that you might not be quite as ordinary as you seem.

Any such impression can be dispelled in an instant by letting your lover catch just a glimpse of a small pistol. It could be buried among maps in the glove compartment perhaps or on the hat-shelf inside your wardrobe.

Not a real one, of course. Mine is a reproduction Browning .765 bought from *Exchange and Mart*. I need something fairly convincing because I also leave it on the hall stand to deter burglars. But any toy gun will do as you won't be holding it up for close examination.

Though some authorities refer to the tactic as 'Bonding' after the fictitional secret agent, it would be an error to dismiss it as far-fetched. A mature adult is hardly likely to have a concealed firearm unless there was a need for it. And the slighter your personality, the more your secret possession will intrigue.

It's been shown (Sherwood Policy Group, 1958) that women succeed with gun play more often than men.

The Attraction of the Right Injury

Though this is really an extension of the personality incentive above, its importance, I think, merits its own section. Since ancient times the injury has had romantic associations with chivalry and honourable battle. And this link can be profitably translated into sporting endeavour in today's less colourful world.

So if you have a corn or in-growing toenail it pays to attribute the resulting limp to an OK sporting injury. An OK mishap is an accident at rugby, polo or riding, but not soccer, darts or jogging. The proliferation of public courts makes tennis no longer acceptable, but squash just about creeps in as a pastime of proper society.

Similarly a scratch from the cat or a rose tree can be passed off as a fencing incident. Observe how the word 'incident' rather than 'accident' has a more dashing ring to it. Your partner will never consider you've been duelling, but the hazy idea will nonetheless linger on a subconscious level.

The Cash Incentive

You don't need to remind any SuperScrooge that only a fool would jettison a lover who turns out to have more money than was first realized. It's logical therefore that carefully placed signs of wealth will keep your partner by your side for that vital 11-week period ($13\frac{1}{2}$ weeks, Gomez).

My courting students are taught to pay for everything with cash not plastic and to bulk out the few notes they carry into an attractive wad with the aid of newspaper. These counterfeit bundles can also be left 'carelessly' around the home.

Naturally you'll contrive to make your lover always call for you in her car. (A leaf could confidently be taken from the book of cousin Tony who falsely claimed he was banned from driving after speeding a sick child living next door to hospital.) But occasionally you can infer a high income by travelling by bus for the major part of the journey to her address, then hailing a taxi for the last half mile. This is very effective, of course, if one lives ten miles away or more.

If you are ever caught on a bus, you must casually, though promptly, mention your allegiance to Green politics.

I Didn't Realize You Were a Financial Wizard

Another helpful corrective to any growing suspicion that your fiscal resources are unacceptable has become known by some of my adherents as 'Absenting the Stockbroker', or 'The Stockbroker Bilk'. But really it's only a variant on the dead phone technique.

While entertaining your target, glance at the financial pages, excuse yourself and make a phone call. Ring any number beginning with 01 (none of these old London numbers will now work). Then ask for a price on Acme gold shares. Pause. Then say, 'I rather thought they might. Please put on £7,000 for me.'

Two or three points to remember here.

(a) Don't offer your name – this will convey that you're known as a regular investor.

(b) Don't buy privatization shares as this kind of popular speculation is rather down-market and tacky and is often associated with financial novices. It might also offend your lover politically.

(c) Only pretend to *buy* shares over the phone. To sell them may give the impression that you're desperate to save your sinking fortunes.

The Jealousy Incentive

A certain measure of risk attaches itself to this next set of ideas for keeping a profitable, nay loving, relationship intact. But as it's 94.3 per cent sound (Hayling Island Trials, 1963 and 1978) I include it, though tentatively.

Waring's celebrated volume *Practical Envy* states that no one will drop anyone from their affections if a third party appears interested and could be waiting in the wings.

An easy way for a man to implicate 'other women' is to buy a lipstick and treat cigarette ends which he can leave in his car ashtray. A hair grip is another inexpensive prop which can be left on the sofa. The female equivalent is to abandon a slightly whiskered razor blade in the bathroom. It's best to plant it unobtrusively in the waste bin rather than more obviously in a cupboard.

Both sexes can exploit any phone call, be it from the coalman, the Women's Institute or the vicar, to evoke a suspicion that another lover is on the line. A nervous 'sorry, can't talk now' will suffice. But remember to avoid eye contact for at least three minutes afterwards.

If you continue any longer, perhaps adding, 'No, it's absolutely impossible. Ring tomorrow. Yes, it'll be more convenient then', and so on, you'll compromise the ploy's veracity. This is because your real lover will instinctively know that any genuine rival would be cut off within seconds.

Dropping Your Lover Quickly and Without Effort

This art is one of life's essentials. For no matter how much preparation is done, your other half can so easily turn out, behind a veneer of glamour, to be both lazy and impoverished. It's not, after all, inconceivable they were able to deceive by studying Scroogecraft too.

The traditionally painless way to off-load an unsuitable lover is to become so unpleasant that the unwanted partner also loses interest. But, easy though it may seem, the habit of becoming slovenly, unpunctual and insolent takes concentration, otherwise your natural charm as a SuperScroogist will seep through. No, a little subversive help is required.

An uncomplicated little ploy for non-smoking couples is to cultivate a nicotine-stained forefinger. Just one licorice stick sustains this effect for some weeks. A little tobacco ash rubbed into your carpet is a worthwhile extra.

My sister Carolyn enjoyed limited success in this field by profess-

ing an interest in emigration. Significantly her choices were the off-putting areas of Iceland and Northern Belgium.

She began by tossing travel brochures around the living room, almost hidden by household magazines. She talked about her love of space, fresh air, and hand-made chocolates. She was later able to supply even more 'evidence', writing to embassies for details. The crested replies were tucked into a letter rack in the hall.

Menaced by such a forbidding future her undesired swain melted from sight.

But perhaps we should turn to Cary Grant for the ultimate way to halt an unpromising love-match in its tracks. In a film whose title I won't, in the interests of time conservation, bother to look up, Mr Grant pretended to be married.

It's obviously embarrassing, not to say mendacious, to tell someone you've been dating perhaps for months that you're already hitched face to face. So we suggest you make the 'admission' to a few mutual friends and await results. It's a strange thing that though people hesitate to tell good friends, much less acquaintances, about their partners' infidelities, any hidden marital status is usually passed on.

A Marriage of Pure Convenience

Having found and cultivated an ideal partner – hard-working though tolerant of indolence, domestically capable while undemanding of others, and monied yet generous – the time has come for marriage.

Many faint-hearted suitors and suitees have wasted years dithering. Often they end up living together, which is nowhere near as rewarding because they get nothing if the relationship shatters. No, our advice, as long as your partner's assets hold, is to take the plunge.

The Ring Recycle

The expense and effort of buying an engagement ring is eliminated if the groom says, 'That sort of thing's a bit old-fashioned now, isn't it?' Actually, it's not, but you're only asking.

He could also talk wistfully about the importance of family tradition. This, it turns out, means that it's nice if engagement and wedding rings can be passed down through the family. And did grannie leave a wedding ring, perhaps?

The bride could also save a lot of trouble – and be trendy – by wearing the wedding dress once worn by her mum or grandmother. They probably had identical figures at that age.

A Good Reception

The bride's father will want to choose the reception venue. He'll pick out some hotel with a reasonable room with a reasonable buffet menu which will just about get by without losing face on the one hand or too much money on the other.

This is a universal truth whether he is stiff with money or impoverished. He'll show you the facilities before a deposit is paid.

The couple must neither criticize the room nor praise it, but should show no reaction whatsoever. They should maintain at least a minute's silence before talking perfunctorily about the weather. When asked specifically if they like the reception area they should reply brightly, but not exactly eagerly, 'Of course. It's fine.'

In the car on the way home the soon-to-be-weds should keep saying alternatively in different ways, 'I'm *sure* it will be all right' and, 'Of course it's absolutely fine.' They should not praise anything specific, or if they do, it should be about something irrelevant, such as the view from the window.

This will, of course, perturb the father who will begin to feel his choice of reception venue is cheap and inadequate. After a day or two, to allow those doubts to mature, the couple should suggest their own hotel at at least twice the expense. This is also the correct moment psychologically to request those little extras, a horse and carriage, Bollinger, celebrity vocalist and motor-boat for transport to the cruise liner.

This eagerness to accede to almost any request, after being humbled into feeling mean, is known among serious exploitionists as Perry's Phenomenon. Needless to say it's adaptable to many more situations than just weddings.

A Wedding is Arranged (by Others)

The groom certainly, but also the bride should leave all the arrangements in other hands. By a show of perpetual nervousness from announcement of the engagement to the day itself, you can assume the cloak of dithering ineptitude. Every performer in the marriage circus will now be eager to help out: parents, bridesmaids, Best Man, ushers, girl friends, best pals, colleagues and neighbours.

A small adendum to this important area of pre-marriage energy-saving is to claim to have read a book on how to be a matron-of-honour. You can then invent all sorts of hitherto unknown duties, from making a hairdresser's appointment for the bride to buying her weekly groceries. A mythical book on 'The Perfect Best Man' would serve a similar purpose. And parents on both sides can be landed with a few hitherto unknown duties too.

Finally

The wedding itself and the immediate aftermath were adequately covered by strategies outlined in earlier SuperScrooge revelations and deserve no further elaboration here. But I have one afterthought to add about the reception.

It's usual nowadays to stage a discotheque-style party to round off the happy day. This is very upsetting for the bride and groom who're expected to depart on honeymoon while everyone else enjoys themselves. May I suggest you announce that, so you can be present, the disco will now take place when you get back. On return, of course, you can resort to Monk's Delay, i.e. you forget all about it.

Shopping and Other High Street Forays

> When you are skinning your customers, you should leave some
> skin on, so that you can skin them again.
>
> —*Nikita S. Kruschev*

DURING the day, the average town-centre bustles, it thrives. By evening it's quite dead. This is because nine to five-thirty shopping is now indisputably the chief outdoor pursuit of the nation. Most of us would be lost without a weekly, if not daily buying jaunt, even though we know our money is sucked away in exchange for things we could mostly do without.

It's an indication of the victory of attraction over necessity, where shopping is concerned, that few of the hoards which patrol our high streets actually seem to buy anything. Nobody totters about under the weight of beribboned boxes any more like Doris Day used to do in romantic comedies. Few, indeed, carry plastic bags. Most are empty-handed. Window-shopping rules.

As SuperScrooge devotees approve of any show which doesn't have an entry fee, one can hardly frown on shopping as a sport. But in this section we can, and do, highlight the correct approach to the little shopping we have to do from a time-effective perspective. This, we submit, is of use to those nipping out at lunchtime and to those like traffic wardens, police officers, bank managers, lawyers, in fact anyone who combines personal shopping with duty.

We also include a few retaliation techniques for getting back at superior or swindling shop-keepers and bringing to book less-than-savoury mail order firms.

Saving Time in Supermarkets

To give supermarket firms some due, they invest heavily into check-out gadgetry to save time, though not quite as much as they do into making us buy unhealthy foods our bodies don't want (see The Supermarket Racket in *SuperScrooge One*).

Of course these chains have an ulterior motive: the faster they can urge us through the tills the more money they take. But it's all a lot better than waiting for a shop-keeper to fetch our needs from behind the counter one item at a time.

This is too advanced a work to proffer tips like stocking up at a supermarket just once a week and buying early in the morning when customers are thin in the aisles. We leave the obvious to our rivals and self-help articles in magazines. But before we progress to some of the more challenging techniques, we'll pause at one of the basics, frequently overlooked . . .

The Fastest Check-out Cashier Around

Most of us make the mistake of joining the shortest line in super-markets, banks, post offices and rail stations, only to find that everyone else moves along five times as fast. A shrewd observer avoids this problem by sizing up not the nature of the queue, but the cashier.

Older employees are likely to be more experienced. Cashiers seen waving goods in the air for confirmation of prices are likely to be beginners. Those who cheerfully chat to customers slow things up.

You should therefore choose a till manned by a frail, beyond middle-aged person with a face as grim as death.

Pushing into A Supermarket Queue (The Toad in the Hole)

This is a way of infiltrating a check-out queue without attracting attention. Put a few things in the trolley. Place it at the back of a queue for the cashier in the normal way. Then appear to have forgotten something and rush back among the shelves to get it. Return with the bulk of your shopping.

Meanwhile your trolley has been pushed forward to keep its place in the line by the shopper behind you. This variation on the per-petual motion rule applies for two reasons:

(a) It requires slightly less brain power to move wheels forward than sideways or climb over them.

(b) Britons will take almost any action to oblige a stranger and thus avoid a possible row in public – especially if a near-empty basket makes them think they will not be delayed too long.

The Fools on the Till

My next trick is so rudimentary that it was almost excluded, but as research shows that few people use it, and the time saved is always substantial, here – with apologies to my more advanced students – it is.

The smallest queue in the store is for the till marked 'for less than ten items only'. So simply hide a few things under an upended large flat box, containing cornflakes, say, and smuggle up to twenty items through at a time. By the time the cashier realizes the ruse the till will have registered a few sales, and it's too late to abort the transaction.

A variant is to use the 'cash-only' till. Once the tally has been made you can whip out your cheque book and apologize for not spotting the signs.

That's Not the Ticket

Research by students of SuperScroogecraft in Rotherham, supported more recently by work at King's College, Mabelthorpe, demonstrates that there are only two reliable reasons why anyone in a serving capacity feels the urge to get a move on on a customer's behalf. The first is a plea by a mother-to-be that she's likely to give birth at any minute, the second is the urgent need to catch a plane.

My manicurist was able to jump a huge queue at the bank when her waters broke over the floor. Though she was certainly pregnant at the time, it was said by some who knew her that she performed a conjuring trick with a bottle of lemonade to speed her transaction – and that her son, Robin, was born two months later as planned.

For those who baulk at such underhandedness, or who aren't with

child, the catch-an-aeroplane gambit is much the more convenient way to jump a supermarket, or any other kind of queue and get away with it.

It's no bad thing when working the Flying Tackle, as it's become known, to produce a prop, viz an airline ticket. This will of course add weight to your claims on immediate service to reach the air terminal in time.

If you haven't travelled by air recently two courses are open. Bus tickets from the National Coach Company look very much like those used by British Airways while other look-alike air tickets are sold by high street travel shops acting as agents for British Rail. N.b. ordinary British Rail tickets will not do.

Fortunately it won't occur to a supermarket cashier to check if the ticket has been used or not. Or in fact to wonder why someone urgently bound for Zanzibar or wherever is in sore need of rhubarb chunks in Buy-Trite anyway.

Jumping the Queue in a Smaller Shop

The trail of customers which often builds up in those shops with a fast turnaround like a confectioners or a fruiterers invariably approaches from the right. You should come at the counter from the left, while pretending not to notice the other shoppers. The assistants, always harrassed in the rapid service trade, will be too busy to spot your 'error'. And the other customers, being British, won't make a scene.

A Stand for Delivery

We've all eased out of the habit of expecting a shop to deliver what we buy – unless our purchase is bigger than we are. But if you gather a box of groceries, there's no harm in asking if it can be brought to your door. Small shopkeepers will do any amount of crawling to please customers nowadays.

As always, the right sort of expression is useful should there be hesitation over the request. A knitting of the forehead by bringing the eyebrows together while forcing the eyes as wide as possible (Smallwood's Look) expresses the sort of anxiety that you may be mugged if you struggle with the groceries yourself.

By way of an amusing aside, I once asked the Greek owner of my local off-licence if they'd deliver my weekly order of champagne. Certainly, he said. I gave my address and walked home. At the gate I turned round to find I'd been followed for half a mile by a large box with a five-year-old child struggling underneath. I felt rather humbled as he carried it down the steps to my wine cellar.

Faster Service in Large Stores

If you find yourself in a long queue in the underwear section of a large store, see if you can spy a less-attended counter in a different department. Though few realize the fact – and staff do their best to hide it – money can normally be accepted anywhere in the store.

Off the Cards

Time-savers only shop with real money. Apart from being faster you can get at least five per cent off for cash almost anywhere (this being the credit card company's commission). And if you flash a wad of notes, suitably bulked out with newspaper, managers will knock great chunks off retail prices to get their greedy hands on it.

Anti-sales Talk

Sales people go on long courses and read dozens of books to learn wiley tricks to make you order what you don't need. Determined to counter this formidable force, my friend Michel began the British Institute of Non-Buying in Manchester.

To save you wasting a fortnight on his expensive tutorials on how to repel pushy sales staff, his primary ideas are published here.

Primary Approach

Look shabby while shopping. This signals your deep reluctance to buy not just new clothes, but almost anything.

Try the three Vs. Appear vague, vacant and vapid. A useful glazed expression is achieved by looking not into the saleswoman's eye, but at a spot two inches above her left eyebrow. Professional sellers seek their first spark of interest in the punter's pupils and if there's no sign whatsoever they'll soon give up.

Advanced Approach (or Going Existential)

As those subjected to sales patter are generally subdued and flat-tened by the experience, sales people don't expect their victims to be bright, breezy and boisterous. So sparkle. Talk a lot, loudly. Don't let the salesman get a word in. Be more enthusiastic than he is – though on any subject other than what he's selling.

The sales pitch may appear spontaneous, but it's engineered step by step to match your mood which is assumed to be rather serious, if not glum. Your totally unexpected show of breeziness, unencoun-tered in any salesman's text book, will throw this prepared routine into chaos. It'll snap the salesperson's concentration and destroy all confidence.

Michel tells me that some hardened professionals have been so democratized by the existential technique that they've found other jobs.

HOW TO INVEIGLE OTHERS INTO DOING YOUR SHOPPING

The Bogus Deal

This section is not without importance as it embodies a major aspect of Scroogecraft: contriving to make others do your work. One ploy at the simple end of the range is played during a call at the iron-mongers, say, with another household member.

All you have to say is, 'It's a bit of a rough old area. If you like, I'll stay and look after the car while you get the things we want.'

Deliberate use of the clause 'if you like' suggests that you're prepared to do someone a favour. You might even seem slightly heroic by preparing to linger in 'a rough old area'.

Your companion will feel that he'll have the best of the deal, though in fact he'll have to hump some heavy stuff about and pay for it, while you languish in warm comfort listening to the car radio.

The One-sided Favour with Barney's Variation

Another admittedly primitive but rewarding tactic is to ask a relative, colleague or neighbour who's about to go shopping to buy something for you while he's about it. Stamps from the post office, winnings from the bookies, that sort of thing. As always with this style of 'plea gambit', laying claim to a minor ailment will help.

Over a few months you'll save a considerable amount of time like this. And you can appear to reciprocate these favours, without actually doing so, by occasionally calling out, 'I'm just going to the shops, does anybody want anything?' This is best done halfway through the door, so nobody has time to consider if they need anything or not.

My cousin Barney feels it safer to slightly change the wording to, 'I don't suppose anybody wants anything?' But my experience is that people hate you to assume anything about their wishes, and their unwanted response to Barney's question might well be 'Yes'.

A cruel example of this particular perversity of thought was when I vainly tried to cut down the expense of my round in the pub (on October 8th, 1978). This was when I asked, 'I don't suppose anyone wants another drink do they?' There was a chorus of affirmation that makes my blood run cold to this day.

No matter. Without the bitter taste of this experience I may never have gone on to draw up the celebrated list, 'How to avoid paying your round', first published in *SuperScrooge One*.

The Fast Way to Buy Clothes

The most gruelling shopping chore of all is the selection and purchase of new clothes. For this reason we advise visiting a charity shop in the very best area of town. Though some cynics say this recommendation is made only in the cause of economy (and they sometimes express it more crudely I'm afraid) the real advantage is that, with everything under the same small roof, buying in charity shops saves oodles of time.

However some of my students have asked me to devise an alternative set of strategies to buying clothes without putting in any effort, suspecting as they do that the image of bon viveur, so complementary to Scroogecraft, is compromised by being seen skulking round an Oxfam shop.

The No-taste Advantage

It's easy to get a loved one or a best friend to do your shopping if you profess (in private, naturally) that you've no taste. Or, at least, not the enviable taste they have.

Hence: 'Would you mind buying me a new shirt and tie, Diana? You know how colour-blind I am.' Or: 'Could you get me some really fashionable black shoes? You're so good at that sort of thing.'

The same method can be used for all purchases requiring judgement. Example: 'David, could you possibly get me six rolls of flowery wallpaper from Liberties? You know how utterly hopeless my choice would be.'

Observe the unobtrusive use of indirect flattery, the delicate bolstering of the other's ego. By denigrating yourself, you mildly lionize your unwitting slave.

The No-taste Advantage (Reversed)

In some parts of Britain, notably Cumbria and much of the West Country, No-Taste psychology is often turned around. Thus, 'I'm going to get the wallpaper, darling, because, well, I hate to say it but your choice can be a bit, well, garish can't it?'

This time the 'slave' can be counted on to drive off to the DIY store in a huff to prove the time-saver wrong. Of course this satisfying ploy is not to be tried by those who can't tolerate a frosty atmosphere for up to two days after its use.

Happy Returns

Customer protection laws force the shop-keeper either to give a refund, or replace your toaster if it vibrates from your kitchen table in an eruption of ebony smoke. But he isn't required to give your money back if you simply change your mind – or discover annoyingly that the store down the road sell it for £30 off. So a few Scroogisms must be called into play.

A special two-point thrust has been evolved, which though likened to the alternating hard and soft approach of interrogating policemen is only superficially so.

Soft

The first step when returning your automatic potato scrubber or diamond necklace is to search the shop manager's lapels for a name label. From here on you refer to him (often) by his first name. This leads to the belief that he already knows you personally, though he can't remember from where.

If one or more of his colleagues appear as if from nowhere – as they often do to intimidate aggrieved customers – use their first names too. A certain friendliness between all parties has now been established.

Hard

As negotiations continue you should take the necklace from your bag, 'unintentionally' toppling out at the same time a leaflet picked up earlier at the Town Hall. This is entitled, *Trading Standards Department – Your Rights*.

Still not getting through? Then delve further into your bag as though searching for a receipt or guarantee. As if to relieve the pressure of the bag's interior clutter pull out a book called *Advanced Consumer Law* or *Guidelines for Sentencing Commercial Law-breakers*.

Needless to say these impressive tomes are really pot-boiler novels, covered in brown paper and falsely titled in blue ink. As this is how a busy barrister might protect the reference books of his trade, the shop manager now believes he's crossing swords with a legal expert. The battle for your money back is as good as won. One should never underestimate the persuasive power of this kind of prop which can be used to speed results in hundreds of situations.

Uncle Simon, naturally enough, couldn't resist the temptation to take the bag technique too far. His way of putting store managers in a conciliatory frame of mind was to take from his plastic carrier some earlier shopping of a slightly threatening nature. A kitchen knife, perhaps. Or an axe.

He would absent-mindedly keep his hand on this innocent object as the argument continued. The prepared 'glazed look', described earlier in this chapter was also brought to bear.

Like everyone working in the public arena, shop staff know that one day they'll meet a homicidal maniac, so Uncle Simon usually got his way. Until February 3rd, 1991, when he was cautioned, quite rightly in my view, for using threatening behaviour.

And though he finally eluded the charge, he never did produce a receipt for the 'newly bought' cleaver which led to his arrest. Not surprisingly, as Aunt Lizzie acquired it in Coronation year.

There are, by the way, two useful footnotes to the art of encouraging a shop manager to return money.

> The potency of all the above ploys is enhanced by taking with you a tall companion who, during the debate, should stand no more than 18 inches from the manager. This third party should on no account say anything, but gaze without expression into the distance.

Selected examples can be adapted to soften up shop staff for easier haggling over prices.

How to Complain by Phone

It's hardly original to urge someone duped into buying a piece of rubbish by post to ring up the managing-director whose name should be on the accompanying bumph. It's also impractical because telephone receptionists with many mail order firms are instructed never to deviate from the two standard responses on a laminated card screwed to the desk:

(1) 'I'm sorry, Mrs Brown is at a meeting. Can she call you back?' (She never does.)

Or:

(2) 'I'll put you through. Please wait a minute.' This is followed by, ironically, an electronic chiming of *Onward Christian Soldiers* by the Micro Chipmonks which continues onward until you hang up.

The opening move against this attempted brick wall is to ring either half an hour before or one hour after standard office hours. This is when executives are often at work, while telephone receptionists aren't. The line may well be connected directly to the boss's office.

But if the company is built on shaky ethical foundations, the management won't be taking calls at any time. Therefore a more intricate step is required. The following counter is of medical extraction (though there's no intended link here with doctor's receptionists who're also trained to deny contact between their employer and the public).

When asking for Mrs Brown say, 'It's the hospital here. Would you tell her that her tests have come through?' This message, with its hint of urgency, will be relayed on the spot. Mrs Brown, burning with curiosity, will soon be on the line with, 'Tests, what tests?'

Now it's time to claim that the receptionist must have been hearing things, and launch into your complaint. She will, no doubt, recognize the work of a fellow trickster who won't be put off and personally arrange a reimbursement.

The Hair Tonic

Hairdressers have such a monotonous job that many of them sleep through it. Which is why your hairstyle is probably as depressingly mediocre as everyone else's. To inject some life into your hairdresser, and reap the rewards of an attentive cut, you'll need to grasp basics of the VIP range of tricks.

The aim here is to convince the cutter that you are a celebrity of some kind whose appearance is a matter of professional pride.

Why he will then try so much harder isn't certain, but try he will. While robust scientific results are as yet unavailable, no less than five reasons have been put forward, on an interim basis, by postgraduates working on the problem in Pocklington, East Yorks.

(1) The cutter likes associating with the famous.

(2) He's flattered at being employed by a celebrity.

(3) He hopes to see his work paraded on television.

(4) He expects a show-business tip.

(5) He worries about being sued for making a mess of it.

The primary move in convincing a hairdresser that you're famous, when of course he's never heard of you, is to turn the conversation to your 'TV job'. Nothing is easier because like all hairdressers his opening will be, 'Have you had your holidays, yet?'

You: 'No time I'm afraid. Absolutely no time. The BBC's looking for a new game show. There's a new series of Gardeners' World coming up, and [bored sigh] the controller's got this bee in his bonnet about a mini-series on the life of Gladstone.'

Though you were just waffling generally about some guff you'd read in the salon's copy of *TV World* while you were waiting, the hairdresser is now convinced that sitting in his chair is a very big cheese.

Luckily he won't put you on the spot by asking exactly who you are. This is for two reasons: (a) to do so would show appalling ignorance; and (b) it would certainly offend.

By now some unprecedented effort will be going into your tonsure. But icing can be ladled on the cake by the casual remark, 'I've just signed a three-year contract with Granada.' There's no need to add that if you don't keep up the rental payments they'll take the TV set back.

Transport

At the door of the first-class waiting-room, venerable and aloof, stood the warden of Judas.

Max Beerbohm's 'Zuleika Dobson'

NOWHERE is the art of time-saving more satisfying to the fastidious practitioner of Scroogism that when he or she locks horns with the frustrating business of getting from A to B. From the lowly number 7 bus to intercontinental flights, the seemingly simple task of moving about is bedevilled by smug employees skilled in presenting travellers with difficulty and delay. Their expertise is as imaginative as it is hard to counter. But they can be thwarted if you rely on the SuperScrooge traveller's survival guide, extracts of which are published here for the first time.

Airport Management

We're always ordered to the airport an hour or more before an international flight. Which is no less annoying than being ushered into the Odeon sixty minutes before the film starts.

The airlines say they must allow for difficulties in processing tickets and dealing with baggage. In which case they should stop requiring their employees to take courses in being extra slow. They won't – because the more people there are milling around the terminal, the more perfume, magazines, postcards of aircraft which all look alike and pricey cheese sandwiches that can be sold.

Fortunately, so many sheep-like passengers heed the early call, that the sensible can afford to arrive not much earlier than take-off time. By this time, there'll be no queues to join and someone will actually show you which gate to go through.

Another bonus for the late arriver is that the last suitcase on the plane is always the first off.

However, should you cut too fine your arrival at the terminal, it may be necessary to run up and down escalators and across the crowded concourse. The accepted way to shoo the rabble from your path is to scream as you go, 'Rabies alert! Rabies alert!' It may not mean anything, but it certainly works.

If by some mischance you arrive too early by mistake it's easier than you might think to persuade the ticket desk to put you on an earlier flight – even if a rival airline is involved. They all have reciprocal agreements.

TRAIN MANAGEMENT

How to Counter a Pedant Who Holds Up the Ticket Queue

Even if the line is quite short, there'll still be someone at the front, who's confused about his credit card, the timetable, and the platform number. And then has ten questions about the return journey. The correct approach here is to huff, puff and tut behind this nuisance. Sigh and consult your watch. Exclaim: 'For goodness sake,' while showing general signs of impatience.

If this procrastinating ticket-buyer is a foreign visitor (usually they are) you can take advantage of a curious fact: the more you sound like a Lord or Lady, the more they'll be humbled and stop asking silly questions. Thus, you need to grumble away with aristocratic, if rather old-fashioned, exclamations, like, 'My dear chap!' or, 'I say. This really is the giddy limit.'

No need to worry that you don't look particularly blue-blooded. You'll be behind your opponent all the time.

It's also because you're unseen that an opposite but equal ploy can be brought to bear.

Assume the identity of an East End thug, using phrases like, 'Gor, blimey, John, leave it art,' and, 'Strike a light, wotta plonka.' This sort of thing can sound very threatening coming from behind. Especially when delivered with the right gravelly intonation.

But fight off the temptation to add, 'or I'll rearrange your features,' as this would go down in a policeman's notebook as threatening behaviour.

Dealing with the Ticket Clerk

Once at the head of the queue the game changes. On no account must the clerk suspect you're in a hurry. Service comes much quicker if you pretend to have mislaid your money. You can see the ticket seller's point of view. There's no fun in delaying a customer who's not in a dash to be off.

How to Get to Your Destination Earlier then Expected

No reminder should be necessary, but sadly it is, that the first task on arriving at a station is to check that an earlier train has not been delayed. You might still catch it, even though this contravenes the uncannily reliable Jacobson's Law (colloquial version), to wit: When

any public conveyance is late, the passenger is on time. When a passenger is late, the conveyance is on time.

How to Defeat a Train Queue

The first thing to realize about any kind of queue is that it's a daft British custom which most other nations rightly scorn. As it's not a legal entity, there are no penalties for jumping one. A brave soul will march straight from the back to the front and expect to get service.

In practice a little more guile is necessary – though not all that much is required to jump the queues for trains at large stations like King's Cross. At a signal from a porter, the hitherto well-ordered crocodile decomposes and its individual parts crush forward in a disorderly stampede.

All you need do is to lurk around the ticket-barrier, perhaps tying a shoe-lace or scanning the destination board until this electric moment. Then stride purposefully forward and be first on.

How to Get a Seat in a Crowded Train

Just like airports, rail stations are filled with nervous souls who arrive long before their trains depart. Yet the worry that no sitting room will be left available is groundless. Many seats are reserved for people who never show up. (Though it's not conclusive, studies in Liverpool indicate that many adults claim to be making business trips when in fact they stay in their own town for illicit love trysts.) So people boarding at the last minute can immediately occupy these spuriously reserved places.

If, however, space is at a premium, and you spot another late-comer looking furtively around before attempting to perch on a seat with a reserve ticket, you should say, amiably but firmly, 'Sorry, my seat, I think.' Even if you don't get the authoritative tone quite right (and I do advise you to practise) he probably won't ask you to prove the claim.

Supposing you board a train with very few vacant seats. The first one you come across is not ideal – perhaps the man sitting opposite has a streaming cold – but you daren't leave in case you have to stand for 300 miles.

The correct procedure is to leave your coat or book on the seat and continue the search. If you find a better seat take it, and return later when all the passengers are settled. Don't fret. Your property won't vanish. No thief will steal when he isn't able to get away – and the stealable item is sitting under the noses of two or three other possible owners.

How to Make Another Passenger Give Up their Seat

Should you fail to find a seat away from the fellow with the runny nose, you'll need to make him move away from you. Holding your stomach with one hand while holding a bag to your mouth is as reliable a gambit as any. And it's not that embarrassing, because everyone sympathizes.

For myself, I never travel without my grandfather's old pipe. This is always produced, together with a former sweet tin, discreetly relabelled 'Stoker Jereboam's Black Shag', to deal with over-crowding in non-smoking compartments.

Cousin Barney used to get a seat every time by saying, 'It's not often the six o'clock to Leeds is this crowded,' knowing full well that Hull was the train's real destination. The pronouncement always caused at least one seated passenger to get off. Barney's timing was such that by the time his victim learned the truth the train had departed. However, this trick is extremely mean and earns only cursory admiration from this author.

Avoiding a Familiar Passenger

Here's a common dilemma. You're walking contentedly down a carriage when you spot somebody you can't stand at any price. He's sitting next to an empty seat and motions you to join him. In actual fact this unspeakable prospect is all-too-easily parried. Yet most people do quite the wrong thing.

They'll either sit down politely and endure up to four hundred miles of mental agony, or they'll scuttle past while pretending not to notice. This last action, being a rotten show of bad manners in anyone's language, isn't tolerated in any SuperScrooge creed.

Far better to say, 'So nice to see you, but I can't stop. I'm with a party of accountants at the back of the train. Hard going I'm afraid, but we're going over the firm's VAT returns since 1985. Long job, won't even finish by the time we get to London. . . .'

Another nuisance, which has a parallel situation in restaurants, is when you are looking forward to gossip with an interesting travelling companion. Inconveniently, a familiar bore approaches bent on joining you for the journey.

The defence here is to whisper to your friend, 'Quick, start a row.' Then stage a vitriolic argument, spiced with personal insults and angry gestures. This splendid tactic is based on Redmond's Rule: No third party will join an altercation already in progress.

By way of warning, always be careful with staged arguments. A degree of concentration is required to make sure a few home truths don't slip out. That's when the fake can so easily become real.

Getting a Stranger to Bring Coffee from the Buffet

Really smart time-conservers never leave their seats at all. They wait for the person sitting opposite to rise then say, 'Hurt my blasted foot. If you're toddling to the buffet would you mind awfully? Coffee and egg sarnies please. I'll settle up when you get back.'

That invaluable standby, the invented injury, will move the other passenger to comply whether she actually intended to buy refreshments or not. (Older people should claim rheumatism which is even more effective.)

Some users of this ploy get a rather childish thrill by bounding away full of life when they reach their destination, knowing that they'll never see their victim again, while really keen energy conservers extend the idea to recruit strangers to carry their bags around stations and onto trains.

This is as good a section as any in which to enter an important general note about requesting favours from strangers. There is a tendency among the uninitiated to ask in formal tones. But the earlier favour request beginning 'Hurt my blasted foot . . .' is better because it uses slang expressions, i.e. 'blasted', 'toddling', 'sarnies', 'settle up'. Because these terms have a more intimate feel the stranger won't feel quite so unknown to you. He'll be that much more anxious to please someone who seems familiar somehow.

How to Be the First Off a Train

M. Robinson the physicist once put forward an amusing theory linking brain waves with mechanical motion along a straight line to confirm what all of us know: that the more crucial your meeting the later your train will be. To counter the damaging effects of this curious fact, many business people use the inter-city shuffle. Five minutes before estimated time of arrival, you'll see them stroll through every carriage right to the front of the train.

This saves more minutes than might be expected. You won't have to jostle along the platform with other passengers and you'll steal a march on anyone else looking for a taxi.

How to Improve the Chances of Boarding a Full Bus

You join the end of a long queue and it's likely that the next bus along will be nearly full. There are several appropriate tactics here. Not my personal favourite, because it involves extra effort, is simply to walk on to the stop before yours.

Much better is to inform fellow travellers you heard on local radio that there was a strike at the depot this morning. 'I expect it will all be over by now. You know what these disputes are like.' A large proportion of the queue will drift away.

Another use of false trail strategy is to say, 'It's bad enough the bus being late, but it's bound to be stuck for hours at those big road works ahead of us in Blossom Street.' The people who set off in disgust may never see this imagined disruption, but then again this kind of repair work can often disappear overnight.

How to Run for a Bus

Everyone knows that bus crews alleviate the boredom of driving around the same roads everyday by judging to a T the moment they can pull away leaving a would-be passenger gasping in their wake. But they do have a better nature. And you can foil their base intentions by a subtle appeal to it.

Most people run flat out for a bus, perhaps flapping shopping-bags about to make a more conspicuous figure in the driving mirror. This is the classic wrong approach.

A vital part of a bus driver's job is looking rearwards so he knows perfectly well who is behind. Your last-minute attempts to board should therefore be almost imperceptible.

Begin by loping along quite slowly with just the merest suggestion of a limp. If this is ignored and the bus starts to move, you must stumble and fall. This isn't damaging if done purposely and in slow motion, with correct use of a body roll (see Thornton's *Exercise and Public Transport*, Lilac Press). Now look upwards with despair.

A modification for those who haven't read their Thornton and are wary of the running fall is to drop your shopping all over the pavement.

If the bus continues on its way after all this, you've discovered a real hard case. Note the number and report him for inconsideration to a pensioner (even if you're only 22).

The Walker Variation

My neighbour Michael Walker claims an unblemished record in this field. His gambit is to run two or three steps. Then he staggers to a halt, takes one step back, clutches at the air and finally clasps his heart. Being a real artist he never forgets that this organ is in the middle of his upper chest, not to the left.

How to Steal a Taxi

You'll be aware from the attendant publicity that full notes on how to exploit taxi drivers are given in *SuperScrooge, 3000 Sneaky Ways to Save Money*. But I haven't yet disclosed the approved ways of hailing a cab.

It's pouring. Other potential customers are lurking in the high street. Some cab-users believe that you should wait some yards beyond your rivals because the driver requires time to stop. Quite wrong. Cabbies will always screech to a halt for the nearest person, because the sooner the meter starts the better they like it.

If you get to a cab exactly at the same time as someone else you should gasp out, 'My wife . . . baby . . . emergency . . . do you mind?' Naturally, your competitor will stand aside. But don't forget to name your real destination quickly, otherwise your driver will set off for the hospital.

Supposing a queue has built up in the rank at a railway station or airport and you can't wait. The passenger who's waited stoically until he's at the front will enter from the pavement side. The minute the taxi draws up you should nip in from the off-side.

Adopt the relaxed posture of someone who's been there some time. But look startled, as though your privacy is intruded upon somehow. Not only will the other passenger withdraw, you'll get an apology as well.

Getting a Taxi to Go Faster

The expression 'Step on it, mate' is interesting nowadays only as a historic reminder. 'Put the pedal to the metal' is slightly more acceptable. It might, but this is a long chance, tickle the driver into co-operation.

An offer of 'Ten pounds if we make it by 3 o'clock' is better, but expensive. I recommend instead a technique known to fast movers in the business world as The Grim Reaper (related to the lesser-known Mr Big gambit, details of which follow).

The driver will know you mean business if you slide silently and expressionless into the cab. State your destination and no more. Don't say please or thank-you. Don't smile. Throughout the journey stare sourly, straight ahead. The cabbie now perceives you're someone of importance who knows his way around.

He'll be faintly, inexplicably aware that you must not be crossed, that he mustn't go the long way round and that time is of the essence.

The aforementioned Mr Big gambit wins just a little more respect from the driver, relying as it does on a sense of melodrama, or rather his remembrance of Hollywood crime thrillers. If you want perfect service from your cabbie – and when did you last have that? – you must, by nuances of behaviour, lead him to think of you as a shady, dangerous character. Then he'll be anxious to be rid of you in a hurry. This speeds the journey along famously.

Your manner should ape that of a gangland boss. Sit in the off-side corner of the rear seat so you can watch for following cars in the wing mirror. Eyes should dart from side to side. The hand is tucked Napoleon-like into the jacket. Women should ostensibly refresh their lipstick nervously while seemingly checking for rival assassins in the hand mirror.

You think this sequence is flawed by impracticality? The reason it

Grim Reaper and Mr Big.

isn't is that cabbies in big cities pick up very crooked characters every day; they can afford the fares.

By Tube? – Only When You Know How

A tube train is usually the exact length of the platform. It follows then that the doors open at the very same place every time. I use yellow chalk to mark these magic spots.

But if you're new to that particular platform, look out for bulges in the waiting line of commuters. I'm not the only one who knows where the doors open.

Really experienced tube strategists stand 22 inches to the left or right of centre. This is the ideal position to sidle on from the side while people are still alighting.

The tube train arrives and it's packed like a sardine tin. Don't wait for the next one. Neither should you encourage belligerence by telling people to 'shove up inside'.

Instead say something mildly humorous. Try, 'Altogether now, all breath in,' or, if you're rather portly, 'Any room for a skinny one?' Such good-natured banter breaks the tension making it easier for people to accommodate a stranger.

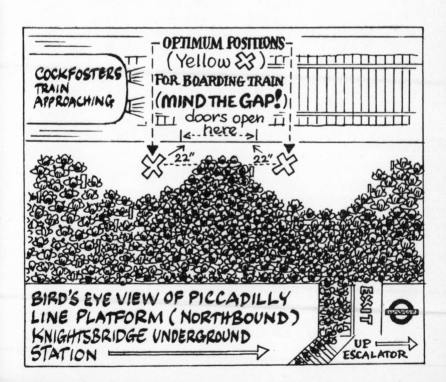

The Car

The only ways to make time while *in* a car is to (a) speed up and (b) take chances. But these exercises are hardly savings if they increase the risk of a mistake which costs you your whole life. There are, however, some ways you can conserve time in the way you prepare for a journey.

Finding the quickest route is a good start. Like everyone else, I'm acquainted with a clever Dick who knows every 'best way' going. I always ring and flatter him into ringing me back with the details. (He likes to make out he knew the shortest route by heart. But I know that before picking up the phone, he studied his maps for an hour to prepare the information.)

If one's travelling with a friend, you can persuade her to drive by brandishing a map and saying, 'The route's rather tricky, perhaps I should do the navigating.' How's she to tell you know the way blindfolded?

Rapid Parking

Most motorists believe that paying for a space in a car park is quicker than looking for a side-street which may be many yards away. How misguided. Once you've taken into account all the palaver of following direction signs, searching for change, buying a ticket, hiking back to your car and sticking it to a non-stick windscreen, the side-road is well worth the extra walk.

Your car is also safer in a residential area. Thieves tend to believe that the owner could be keeping an eye on it from a bedroom window. Break-ins are more common in car parks.

Really cunning parkers always have a stethoscope (mine is actually a toy one) lying around on the rear seat. Then they can park near hospitals.

Easy Car-starting

I conserve a lot of time by not having my car serviced as much as grasping mechanics hassle me to. Occasionally this makes my vintage V8 a beggar to start. Here's how to ensure you don't waste precious moments setting off in the morning:

Keep another battery ready-charged in the garage.
Own a set of jump leads.
Leave the choke out overnight.
Leave the bonnet open and let the wind blow away any
    dampness.
Buy a house on a hill.

Every Motorist Has to Deal With Walking Eventually – the Art of the Short Cut

Supposing you want to go to a park or playing-fields without walking all the way to the gates. There's a row of houses with rear gardens backing onto the park. Merely knock on a door and ask the way. You'll be invited to nip through the back.

Nothing in this book incites readers to break the law, but when you see one of those annoying 'Keep off the grass' signs, the chances are this is nothing to do with a by-law – just a piece of arbitrary repression.

You should cut across the sward if it saves you time. If some official rudely asks, 'Oi, can't you read?' you should quietly reply, 'No [faint dramatic pause] I'm afraid I can't.' As everyone sympathizes with a lack of educational opportunities and it could mean you were an orphan, your accoster will suddenly feel rather small.

Day to Day Existence

The art of pleasing consists in being pleased.
—William Hazlitt

THIS chapter caresses themes which resonate down the ages. It is devoted to demolishing the more common hurdles of everyday living which steal so many hours with so little to show for them. The inconveniences heaped on us by the social demands of other people which eat away at our lives, wasting precious moments. Here's how to take the sting from these inconveniences.

The Quick Way to Letter-writing

It's only true in the crudest sense that for nearly every letter sent, a much quicker phone call would have done. We all thrill to a postman's knock, whereas a ringing phone is often a bit of a shock or an interruption of a favourite TV programme. Letter writers are popular. And popularity wins lots of favours. But though letter-writing is still an essential social grace, worthy SuperScrooge concepts have been devised to reduce the chore.

Rarely is the observance of good manners anything but inconvenient: a small expenditure of energy for no return. But in letter-writing it works for us. Etiquette is seriously breached if we answer a social missive too soon. Quite simply a reply within four weeks is an insult. Haste smacks of a desire to put an unpleasant duty behind us. The correspondent suspects you're writing with little thought.

No, the correct thing is to reply very late. Which of course means writing far fewer letters in the long run.

If you send a personal letter you're rather proud of, save a copy and use it as a model for all future correspondence. Home computer users know how simple this is.

When, in my younger days, anyone sent me a thank-you letter, I noted down the most striking sentences. Later I put them all together to make a message of gratitude stunning in its eloquence. I've economized on brain-power by copying it ever since.

I fear no discovery. It's an odd fact of life that though people sometimes save letters, they never read them again. So incriminating comparisons are never made.

92

Making a Short Letter Appear Long

Here are the classic rules, condensed from my edition of a clandestine guide to publishers seeking to make their slimmer volumes look thicker.

Keep your writing large, your spaces and margins generous. Use lots of paragraphs and write on one side of the shortest but thickest paper. Employ plenty of long dashes and no abbreviations.

Expand words into phrases. For example: 'Here reproduced by way of a truly excellent example', instead of 'for example'. Or:

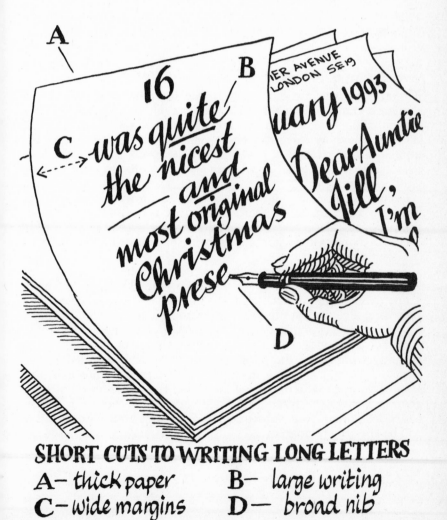

SHORT CUTS TO WRITING LONG LETTERS
A— thick paper **B**— large writing
C— wide margins **D**— broad nib

'Somewhere in the probable region of about £50', rather than '£50'.

The full use of your address can also fill up space. The quite adequate 49 Pigpen Lane, Derby, can be expanded to The Three Laurels, 49 Pigpen Lane, off Sty Lane, Wheatley Hills, Derby, Derbyshire DBU 5XJ. If your house is unnamed you should, of course, make one up (see chapter on acquiring an instant image).

It's also possible to reduce effort by telling your correspondent that you have shingles. Over the next few paragraphs allow your writing to deteriorate. Then you can rapidly sign off after some barely legible squiggles which advertise that you can no longer hold your pen.

Should you correspond with a friend over sixty, averages assert that her memory is unreliable enough to safely accuse her of not replying to a letter you never actually sent. This will force her to the position of having to send two letters to your none. This is a classic SuperScrooge play as it cuts your effort at the expense of hers.

A Quick Response for a Letter of Complaint

It amazes me how just one letter, literate and politely expressed, can change a company's whole policy overnight. As a journalist, I've known whole boards of directors on newspapers reel with concern if just one reader writes in to whinge about a trivial mistake. Like the time I turned over two pages in my notebook and accidentally reported that a motorist had been jailed for nine years for driving with one rear light.

Even so if your written complaint goes to a lowly member of the firm – to complain about poor bus services, say – it may not evince the response it deserves. And even if you write specifically to the big cheese by name, your letter will probably be intercepted by a protective employee.

The way to solve your problem with an indolent company is to write to a minion but to mark the letter with three magic words, 'Copy to managing-director'. There's no need to spend effort actually preparing a copy. Just the belief that you've sent one will goad any obsequious lackey into action on your behalf.

Such correspondence should always include something like, 'A faithful customer of 36 years' standing is surely entitled to expect. . . .' Though this is a metaphorical observation, not meant to refer to yourself who may have only used the bus service once, the assumption will be made that their very best customer has been badly let down. Your subsequent suggestion about compensation will be speedily honoured.

How to Keep a Conversation Short

Bing Crosby said you never learn anything while you're talking. He didn't add that if you're not doing the talking, a lacklustre two-way parley will take only half as long. Actually, being a good listener can make the encounter even shorter. If your conversant doesn't feel his words are sinking in, he'll resort to re-emphasis and repetition. It could go on for ever.

Being a good listener means maintaining eye contact. You should also look concerned, titter at the jokes, go 'um' quite a lot and nod your head. But don't go too far: slapping your knee while declaring, 'Well I'll be damned,' smacks of mockery.

How to End a Conversation Instantly

Traditional Anglo-Saxon methods of looking at your watch and murmuring, 'Well, I must get on' or, 'I expect you're rather busy so . . .' seem only to goad the other speaker on. There is only one way to terminate a tedious conflab; that's to clap your hand to the side of your face, say, 'Help. There's something vital I've forgotten to do,' then run out of the room.

Removing Someone from a Telephone Box – The Problem

Right up there in the elite of annoying everyday incidents is arriving at a public phone kiosk to find somebody already in there. Not only is the bounder chuckling away, which means there's no sense of urgency about him or his call, but he's adjacent to a tower of coins which also portends a long wait.

The necessary task of eviction is fraught with difficulty. Tap gently on the glass or open the door to ask politely, 'Will you be long?' and you'll only irritate the caller into turning his back and digging in. Pace about impatiently or loom menacingly over the kiosk and you'll get the same result.

Uncle Lesley, who's 6 ft 2 in and often has to put late bets on, was, and is, very successful at growling, grabbing the culprit under the arms and lifting him out into the street. Though we grudgingly admire him, such lack of finesse can have no official approval here. So what *is* to be done? Well, NATS (The National Association of Time Savers) recently formed a think-tank to formulate official responses to this key problem and some of their early work is promising.

Removing Someone from a Telephone Box – The Solution

NATS believes that it's a fallacy that only poor people use phone boxes. Most public callers arrive by car, sometimes because their own phone is out of order, or because they want to call illicit lovers. So you can press a piece of paper to the glass saying, 'Beware, traffic warden about.'

Naturally, this won't work if there are no yellow lines in the vicinity. In this case write, 'Suspicious character round your car'; or, if the incumbent is bedecked in trouser clips or luminous arm bands, '. . . round your bike'.

Should the caller be a younger teenager – how often they are – naked bribery is in order because at this age it's cheap. An offer to 50p to postpone their call for you to make yours is usually accepted.

Whether you pay up afterwards depends on a difficult question of morality. You might feel, as I tend to, that exposing the young to bribery is wrong and an early example that it doesn't pay, and that bribers sometimes welsh on the deal, is justified.

Another ploy to empty a telephone box of its garrulous occupant depends on whether or not you're carrying a bottle of mineral water in your shopping. If you are, why not pour some on the pavement so it trickles gently onto the kiosk floor. As the phone-hogger won't know what this liquid really is and will feel uneasy about making a closer investigation, he may well hang up in a hurry.

But the think tank's most effective, and certainly quickest, method for evacuating a telephone box to date is based on misleading word-play, or more accurately, on the use of non-sequitur.

You pull open the kiosk door, gasping, 'There was an accident . . . Someone very hurt.' Then, while snatching the handset and fumbling in your pocket, ask, 'You don't have to put money in to dial 999, do you?'

The phone-user will now make three assumptions: (a) There's been a horrific road smash; (b) someone is seriously injured; and (c) you want to dial an ambulance.

But all you really referred to happened thirty-two years ago. That was when you stepped on your brother's squeaky rabbit (accident) and he was upset (very hurt). After this your conversation changed tack to make a casual enquiry about whether the public must pay to ring 999.

So far so good. But then our experts had to address a problem. Though your opponent will give up the phone immediately, he may still hang around. They decided that if you want to make a longish call, you can get rid of the former caller by blurting out, 'Quick, it's over there,' while making a very vague directing gesture. He'll then charge away to the 'accident' to give help.

Being unable to find carnage, he should be away for some time. If he comes back unexpectedly you could explain that he misunderstood you, but five out of seven on the think tank feel, on the whole, it's best to run off.

How Not to Be Punctual

Theoretically, there are few better ways to preserve time than to be ten minutes late, especially for business or social dates you don't relish. This, however, sours your reputation as a considerate person.

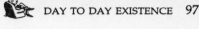

The way out is to arrive five minutes early for your *first* meeting with each person you have dealings with because, 'I always like to be on time, it's only fair.' And once your reputation for punctuality is established you can arrive late thereafter and get away with it every time.

Making a Flying Visit

This addition is to aid those of you with selfish relatives who have to be visited (perhaps for a quick loan when you're suffering a fiscal reality gap) but lack the decency to allow you to leave in a hurry.

True, there's still a modicum of mileage left in 'Can't stop. I've got a taxi waiting!' But, as students of the SuperScrooge Way, you'll be anxious, I know, to avoid even effective ideas if they've become clichés. So allow me to subscribe a few more imaginative moves.

The swiftest way to complete a visit is not to visit at all, but to crouch low and sneak up on the letterbox with a prepared note. Hence: 'I missed the Boat Race by coming to see you today, but there was nobody in. My own fault, I should have phoned first.'

Reference to the 'Boat Race' (or any strategic big event that day) serves a useful purpose. It could mean that you generously denied yourself a day out in London to see your aunt in Birmingham, or even that you now live in the south and made a special trip for nothing.

Actually you'd sort of toyed with the vague idea of watching the race on TV from which a little of the atmosphere might just percolate.

You won't get your loan then and there, but no doubt the relative, who probably blames deafness, real or imaginary, for missing your knock will ring you to apologize. You can now raise the matter of cash.

An ancillary benefit of this ploy is that the planned visit and a vulgar request for money are less likely to be connected.

But not all experts agree that the Non-Call, as it's become known, is worthy of this volume. The general dissent, led by my brother Richard, can be traced back to his 1986 visit to Great Aunt Beatrice in Henley-on-Thames.

Richard followed the rules exactly – he claimed to be missing the Grand National. He was in crouched position, ducking beneath the glass window in the front door, when Great Aunt Bea coincidentally opened up to collect the milk.

Having had the presence of mind to claim he was suffering acute rheumatism, Richard endured a wretched two hours chatting with our relative while bent double by the fire. As his hostess was genuinely similarly afflicted, they must have made a curious sight.

Secret Short Cuts to Track Down Someone who Owes You Money

The following tips certainly save time and may have more use than you might think at first blush. Both were passed to me by Secret

Service spies of my acquaintance who've been invaluable in the compilation of this work.

Observe, by the way, how you now begin to view me in a more respectful light because you believe I'm in direct contact with the espionage world. In fact the two tricks in question were found in rather tawdry espionage thrillers (Humberside Libraries 1989) and my 'acquaintance' with the spies is in a fictional sense only.

This distinctive style of misleading language is all too often lumped under the catch-all expression 'weasel words'. But it's much more than that. Once thought to have been originated by Victorian detective Catchgrove, this skill of false association has recently been traced back to Etruscan manuscripts. And, of course, once mastered it's invaluable in providing all sorts of qualifications for oneself without actually claiming them.

Returning from this fascinating digression to the promised question of tracking someone down, I direct you to the familiar find-someone-who-lives-in-a-block-of-flats problem. You know how it is, the quarry certainly lives in Barbary Towers, Knightsbridge, but you can't recall the flat's number. There are scores of tenants and an intercom lock bars the way.

The solution, simple when explained, is to ring a dozen bells at the same time. At least one disturbed resident, expecting someone or other, will trigger open the main lock without asking who goes there – and you're on the inside. It's now possible by reading interior name-plates or asking a few neighbours to quickly locate your friend.

A related ingenuity helps those who'd like to call unannounced on hotel guests, but don't know the room number. It was used quite recently by my nephew Simon's choirmaster to confront the felon who welshed on a Derby bet (his own fault for disregarding the on-course maxim: never wager with a man in trainers).

The trick is done by sealing an envelope with the name of your quarry written on the outside. Hand it to the hotel receptionist who'll put it in the guest's pigeon hole. And that will be marked with the room number. Remember it and without asking permission take the lift.

Saving Time at the Ballot Box

Eric Smith, my barber, occasional mentor and Christmas tree supplier, used to boast, to his shame, that as he'd never known an election won by just one vote, he wasn't going to waste shoe leather trudging to the polling station. We didn't, alas, make much headway by asking what would happen if everyone took this view.

No, there is only one responsible way *not* to vote and that's to strike a deal with a neighbour of different political views. I remember from my youth that Tom Swales the miner voted Labour while

The **WRIGHT** & **SWALES** Non-Voting Pact · 1959
A milestone in the Democratic Process—
Differing neighbours agree to **PAIR**...

E. R. Wright, the piano teacher next door, always supported the
Conservative hope. Each agreed not to vote if the other one didn't, as
this way, they reasoned, they would only cancel each other out.

It wasn't until 23 years later, on Tom's death, Mr Wright admitted
to his widow that he used to sneak off to the polls anyway when
Tom was at his working men's club. 'No harm done,' she said, 'Tom
used to go there before you got up.'

The story illustrates nicely how primitive forms of pure Scroogism were performed in the suburbs long before this author codified and recorded the main principles to set out in written form.

The Art of Jury Service Avoidance

Being unwilling to serve with another eleven 'good and true' souls in the cause of justice has been known to strike some critics as irresponsible. Which is why we put the matter to our ethics committee, knowing as we do that (a) its members have some first-hand knowledge of Crown courts and (b) they can truly be described as independent, as three of the eight are somewhat unaccountably barred from serving themselves.

This body decided that as with tax there's a wide difference between EVASION, which is wrong, and AVOIDANCE which is allowable in most circumstances. A case of disappearing to Peru when you know your services are required is 'evasion'. Giving the courts a reasonable cause to reject you as a juror can fairly be described as avoidance.

Some Scroogists have been responsible enough to explain that they shouldn't go in the jury box because they might recognize some of the defendants. Others have mentioned hearing impediments.

On the other hand you might want to write to the courts expressing your enthusiasm for serving on a jury, although this kind of thing can unfortunately rebound, so that instead of sitting through three months on a fraud case, you're forced to get on with your normal carefree life.

Uncle Ernest wanted to sit on a jury. But after writing a letter of acceptance he couldn't understand why the court suddenly went cold on the idea. He later showed me a copy of his words.

Dear Court Official,

I'm really thrilled that at last I've been picked for jury service. Now, after all these years I can really get down to putting the criminals who roam our streets behind bars. These undesirables have for too long been allowed to get away with it by over-lenient courts. They deserve long, long sentences and by golly, I'll make sure they get them. So help me!

Yours sincerely

Ernest Thompson

Personal Finance

But it is pretty to see what money will do.
— *Samuel Pepys, 1667*

Time is money
— *We can't remember who said this*

WOULDN'T you think that with all that investment banks, building societies and insurance companies lodge in computer technology that our financial dealings would be conducted at the speed of light? Isn't it true that money can now be whizzed from continent to continent on wires, credit-worthiness checked in seconds, bank balances verified in moments as computer talks to computer across the world.

Yes, but only in theory. In practice it can still take a high-street bank three weeks to transfer money across the channel to France. A building society takes ten days to clear a cheque.

Of course it's possible to speed up everyday transactions, but it doesn't happen. It now takes even longer to get served at the counter, for a cheque book to arrive and for the paperwork to come through on a new mortgage.

Indeed the only time bankers act quickly nowadays is when they're foreclosing on a business loan or sending off a reminder that you're five pounds overdrawn so they can send a warning letter and charge up to £20 for the 'service'.

But the lightning advantages to the customer of improved electronics have been neutered by red tape and lack of staff. Red tape because the longer banks keep simple transactions in limbo, the more interest they make on our money. And lack of staff because employing people corrodes profits.

How can we make financial institutions respect our time? It's no good making an official complaint. You need to make a withdrawal – of SuperScrooge cunning.

Forcing a Bank to Put More Staff at the Counter

Every day millions of lunch hours across the world are lost forever to banks which keep one teller on duty while hoards of other

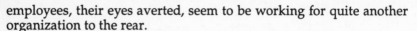

employees, their eyes averted, seem to be working for quite another organization to the rear.

One often wonders if this is a projected film background to lend false credence to the idea that the branch is larger and more important than it is.

The resilient solution to this aggravation begins with a gentle word to the manager. He'll supply the usual reply that all queues are out of his control because he's so very short-staffed. Do not at this stage fall back amateurishly on reminding him of the small army of clerks who seem to be doing nothing of importance behind the counter.

Instead you should sympathize. Say it must be awful. How absolutely rushed off his feet he must be. Then add thoughtfully, 'You know I think I'll write to the top and say how dissatisfied you are ... how really fed up you are that they can't give you enough employees. Can you perhaps give me the chairman's name and the address to send the letter to?'

Not wanting to appear rebellious in a world which abhors rebels, the career-conscious manager will hastily assure you that this is not necessary. Perhaps a few adjustments can be made after all. Maybe it's just a small matter of reviewing the lunch rotas. 'We'll have another look at them.'

You'll know your little tree of cunning has borne fruit when a few days later you get a personal letter from the manager reiterating that there's no need to bring in head office as the shortage of lunch-time counter staff has now been solved.

How to Get VIP Service in a Bank or Building Society

At an early stage in dealings with your local branch it's essential to engineer a very public row. Pick a small grievance. Perhaps you were charged interest in a current account after slipping 50 pence into the red.

Begin quietly with a counter clerk saying you don't think you should pay. It doesn't matter how conciliatory the reply, you should gradually escalate the argument, finally flying into a towering rage.

Unpleasantness is the key word from this point. Each time the cashier speaks, interrupt, sneer, and bang your passbook down on the counter. Be sarcastic and inconsolable. Storm off before concessions are offered.

The purpose behind this deliberate show of fury is that bank staff dread customer outbursts. They're taught to project friendliness at all times; to mask the banking world's fundamentally unkind and grasping motives, by being extra polite.

Because this sort of ugly scene goes against the grain with bank employees, conditioned to blandness, your mercurial temper will be discussed and remembered by the entire staff. Some very careful attempts will be taken never to cross you again.

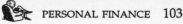

From now on the bank will recoil from bouncing a cheque, writing an expensive letter about your growing overdraft or refusing a loan. You can now revert to your normal charming self (as outlined in the chapter on An Attractive Image – How to Acquire One Instantly) because they'll never be quite certain when this embarrassing passion will erupt again.

How to Receive Star Treatment in a Building Society

The ploy above is like so many of our devices in that, rather like the equalizing pull of matter and anti-matter, there is a diametrically opposed course of action which also has its uses. Indeed this alternative is even more valuable in building society branches, often less welcoming than banks, where just a few easily bored clerks actually relish a counter row now and then.

The trick here is to open your ears to behind-the-counter banter so you learn everybody's first names. Then you can address the counter staff with a show of cheerfulness: 'Hello, June. Haven't seen you for ages. Have you been on holiday?'

You will have also memorized the first name of the manager from the branch notice-board, so you can add, 'How's Adrian by the way? Has he lost any more hairs lately?'

This last question is a personal favourite as it fits almost any condition a stranger may be in while suggesting that you have intimate knowledge of that condition. In other words it erroneously implies that you and the stranger are friends.

This is because 'lost any more hair?' could refer to:

(a) Impending baldness.

(b) A volatile temper.

(c) Illness – the side effect of a drug.

(d) A misfortune befalling an amateur naturalist.

You'd be very unfortunate if at least one of these references did not fit the building society manager. And even if not, the teller will still think you're privy to some part of his private life even she doesn't know about. Which means you must be quite a friend of his.

And make no mistake, personal friends of building society managers always get deferential treatment from underlings in a profession riddled with naked ambition.

How to Beat the Queue at Hole-in-the-Wall Machines

Perhaps it's because mechanical money dispensers are speedier than human ones that they attract more customers who build up even longer queues. In any event there's always a tribe of grumpy customers willing to try their luck in a lengthy line which flows like glue.

To disperse this crowd one needs an idea no less worthy because of its stark simplicity. Address the first in line thus: 'Be very careful before you risk it. It nearly swallowed my card earlier on. And the two cards after mine disappeared altogether.'

It's tempting to continue, 'If you lose your card, you won't get it back and it could ruin your weekend,' but this would be over-egging the pudding.

When the customer wavers you can suggest, 'Let's just try mine one more time'. In it goes and as there was nothing wrong with the dispenser in the first place your transaction will go ahead as normal. Few will notice that you've actually jumped the queue, and those that do will, without really knowing why, be rather grateful.

Getting the Better of the Revenue

It has to be admitted that one of the very few snags of an adherence to Scroogism is that it attracts too much attention from tax investigators. They can't understand how followers with limited incomes manage to live the life of Riley. As these officials deal with many who can't pay their taxes because they've been profligate, they find it hard to grasp that people who've learned the art of not paying for anything, goods or services, will become wealthy.

At one happy stage this unjustified probing was of no consequence. That was when tax officials of quality were thin on the ground because at every chance the real financial wizards of Her Majesty's service deserted in scores for well-paid jobs in the City. But now these opportunities are gone tax investigators stay on, getting craftier all the time. And isn't it likely that their promotion depends on how much money they can claw back?

Their powers are growing too. If they find you owe £1,000 more than you paid one year, they can assume, without proof, that you've worked the same evasion for the last eight years and so claim £8,000. They can also go back to 1937, worryingly before the birth of mainstream Scroogism.

Despite unstinting effort by our 'difficult problems' think-tank over the last eleven months, we've only come up with one general tactic to keep these eager beavers at arm's length and so save days of fruitless hassle. That is to declare absolutely everything by way of income, but make sure you claim every possible out-going too. It's a crime to underestimate your profits, but there's no bar to claiming almost everything you like. A lot of your 'expenses' will be discounted, but some will slip through. Especially if your list is long and the inspector's eyes begin to tire.

Uncle Ernest did once hazard a way, unapproved by our tax avoidance authorities, to explain to the Revenue why his lavish

lifestyle bore no relation to the figure on his tax return. He professed to his persecutors that he never made real money as a high street hatter as he couldn't help donating his wares to elderly ladies of low income. Unfortunately the excuse of being too kindly didn't sit happily with his later exposure by the local paper for operating part-time as both an estate agent and a loan shark.

The Revenue couldn't accept that an estate agent could be quite so magnanimous.

Any reader with uncomplicated tax affairs, including those on PAYE, should send off a letter saying, 'I think I may have been paying too much over the last ten years. Can you investigate?' You may get a fat cheque.

VAT – Two Contrasting Views

Every three or four years VAT payers have a home visit from an inspector to check the books. There are two opposing schools on how to behave on this occasion:

(a) Present the accounts in perfect order in comfortable surroundings.

(b) Show accounts which are correct, but are arranged in a system unique to yourself. Make sure they're not in chronological order. Let the inspector peruse them in an unheated room. Give him a back-breaking chair. Don't offer a cup of tea. Bore him with pointless anecdotes about your business set-backs.

Supporters of method one say an inspector who's kept happy will be less inclined to draw attention to mistakes and won't exact costly penalties, whereas an irritated official might be.

Opponents of this view say it's better to delay and inconvenience the inspector so he's keen to leave as soon as possible. As most go directly home after an inspection, they argue, any delay will eat into his own time. A hurried inspector won't take time to winkle out any mistakes.

Some hard-nosed practitioners of method (2) will attempt to dismiss the VAT inspector in an even shorter time by pretending to be infectious with flu or by giving imprecise directions to make him arrive at their home later than expected. This of course is not a respectful way to treat a public servant.

When entertaining a VAT inspector, special attention should be paid to mode of dress by certain tax-payers – including actors, TV personalities and models. As it's just possible to reclaim VAT on smart clothing deemed to be necessary for a job, it's advisable to appear, when the inspector calls, like a dirty old tramp.

Dealing with Some Inconveniences of Being Short of Cash

Though one's always instinctively disappointed in members of our little band who run short of money, and they're often rather frostily advised to return to SuperScrooge basics to begin again, it has to be admitted that these things can happen, at least temporarily, to the best of us.

Take the everyday happening of a current account which falters into the red. You want to post a cheque, but it may bounce. The procedure here is to borrow a cheque from a colleague and pay him the money direct.

Quite the fastest way to arrange a commercial loan is at one of the growing number of pawnbrokers. Time was when only the very poor patronized these worthies, but now it's considered rather smart to be seen emerging from beneath the three balls. One can even suggest that you're such a walk-on-the-wild-side investor that your vast fortune is currently too wrapped up in shares to allow easy access to even a pound or two.

Your Health

They answered as they took their fees,
there is no cure for this disease.
　　　　　　　　　—Hilaire Belloc

IN every stage of indisposition, from being slightly under the weather to the tragedy of serious illness, we are at the mercy of professionals unrepentant at treating our time with maddening indifference. Casualty departments, hospital clinics, the waiting rooms of doctors, dentists, opticians, chiropodists, osteopaths, even vets are meccas for needless hanging about. Perhaps it's generally believed that time is a great healer, but this is ridiculous.

It's not as if the misfortune of being ill doesn't make its own huge demands on our time. Weeks, months, years are lost to incapacity. Expecting us to wait for treatment adds insult to injury (or illness).

This chapter won't improve your health but it will build up your immunity to medical time-wasters.

It Shouldn't Happen to a Doctor

GPs are fond of telling their patients not to visit them if they can possibly avoid it. Take them at their word and make them come to see you. That way you won't have to risk the barrage of bugs always lurking in their surgeries.

You may have to overstate your symptoms to bring a doctor out on a storm-tossed Saturday night. But why not? They get £32,120 a year to do it.

There'll be those who say this is an irresponsible tactic, as the doctor might need to attend a more urgent case. Don't worry. Life and death cases are rarer than you think. And he can easily be diverted to the real emergency by radio phone. You may even have eased the situation, because at least the doctor is now on the road with a bag packed.

The Doctor's Waiting and Waiting and Waiting Room

Don't bother with the doctor if you get a cold or even flu if you're normally fit. He can do nothing about it. People who say, 'I had some

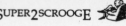

antibiotics and the cold went' are talking tripe. Nothing can beat the cold virus. Run-of-the-mill backache also seems out of the doctor's control so don't waste an afternoon at the surgery on that either.

If, however, you develop anything unusual consult a doctor. Don't worry about taking up his time, once you get in the surgery he'll start wasting yours. Just like the magazines, these places are in a time warp. Why is it, for instance, that I spend less than 45 seconds with an impatient doctor, while the three people before me always take ten minutes each?

Jumping the Surgery Queue

As usual Scroogism is well suited to manipulation, and surely a classic test of that particular craft is to be made by jumping a line of patients at the GP's surgery.

The manner in which this is achieved is to 'mistake' the first name you hear called out for yours and walk quickly and confidently into the doctor''s lair. A surgery is one of those locations where a meek attitude is universally adopted – as opposed to a supermarket or motorway where aggression rules – so you won't be challenged.

The chap whose name was called, who presumably isn't feeling his best, thinks he might just have misheard the name and will stay seated. The doctor won't care either way. But he should be informed that you're not the patient he expected otherwise you could end up with open-heart surgery for a sprained thumb.

The Cure?

A recent survey for *Surgery Monthly* showed that in just one week 37 per cent of patients were identically told by their doctor to 'take this prescription and go to bed for a few days. You've caught a bug and there's a lot of it about.'

This means, of course, that none of these medics had a clue what was wrong and the pills prescribed were placebos – in other words serious-looking tablets which are in fact coloured sugar. Many patients, it's argued, feel better for taking 'something' even if there's no effective ingredient in it.

If you agree that this sounds like faintly insulting bunkum, you should ask your GP directly if you're being palmed off with a placebo or not. If so, you'll save time and money handing the prescription back.

Our Casual Casualty Departments

There's a fallacy abroad (and here too) that the emergency department in a hospital will act like lightning to treat any mishap. This leads victims of accidents to charge straight round to casualty, whereas they'd often be better off calling their own GP. Of course, the overworked medical teams do the business immediately if your life is in danger, but if you're merely in agony from a slipped disc or a crushed foot, prepare for the long wait.

How Not to Be a Casualty of the Casualty Department

One way to speed things up is to wait for a nurse to pass, then slump unconscious at her feet. More experienced time-savers would, however, dismiss this ploy as unreliable. In fact, research at one of Britain's largest hospitals shows that seven out of ten nurses would merely carry out cursory reviving therapy and restore you to the queue.

A cleverer way of becoming a priority in a casualty clinic, or any hospital department, is known as Warner's Way, named after the brother-in-law of the Glaswegian tomato-grower who devised it. This technique, which relies on the form you complete when you agree to treatment, exploits the usual doctor's weakness of snobbery.

All that's necessary is to put down an occupation which impresses. Bishop and MP are good examples. Professor will overawe young student doctors, while Barrister could frighten a doctor into worrying that any delay on his part could result in his being sued for negligence.

Mr Warner's brother-in-law earned his reputation by writing civil servant on his form, later hinting to a consultant that he helps to vet the Queen's birthday honours list.

The Leader of the Plaque

Dentistry is an unusual profession in that a few of its practitioners like to make work. One or two have been officially ticked off for filling healthy teeth. They can be very keen on doing remunerative bridge work. One I saw in London even suggested my false tooth on a plate should be replaced by a bridge, otherwise I might swallow it and die. As bridgework takes forever, and emotional blackmail is recognizable, I decided to risk it.

If your molar mechanic detects a bit of decay ask if his attentions can't really wait until your next check-up in six months' time.

How to Get the Dentist to Pull A Finger Out

One of the commonest paradoxes SuperScrooge is asked to solve is the dentist who keeps sending postcards every three months asking you to have a check-up, but can never fit you in if you have toothache. Not for nothing is my own dentist known throughout Yorkshire as Edward the Unavailable.

If you are in agony, the solution is not to ring for an appoint-

ment which could be in the far future, but simply turn up, preferably with artificially tear-stained face, and state that the pain is so bad you refuse to leave.

This declaration must be made in a loud whisper so that everyone in the waiting-room can hear. No dentist will turn you away. He can't afford to upset his scheduled patients with a show of callousness. Some of them may be private.

You can draw even more attention to your plight if you tie a white bandage around your head from jaw to crown, flamboyantly knotted at the top. Perhaps a wodge of cotton wool could be inserted into one cheek.

The whole surgery will be impressed by this, as it's only ever been seen before adorning toothache sufferers in comics and cartoons.

The dramatic bandage routine is also recommended for ordinary appointments. Fellow patients will urge you to go in first if you're in such a state.

Hospital Visiting at the Double (Without Causing Offence)

A wide cross-section of the public, interviewed by my Uncle Ernest between races at Ladbrokes Office in Great Portland Street, indicated that the most difficult task in everyday life is keeping the conversation going during hospital visiting hours.

And even though the patient yearns for company, it must be remembered that it's exhausting, and therefore recovery-threatening to expect him to keep fighting these embarrassing silences. Here then are four approved stratagems for cutting down an hour's bedside vigil by at least 50 minutes.

If you yawn once or twice, the patient will too. Now you can say with genuine anxiety, 'You're looking very tired, I think I'd better go.' If he protests deepen your concern and call a nurse.

Less subtle perhaps, but less likely to meet with resistance from the patient is to suddenly recall you left the gas cooker on.

My third tip rests on the weather forecast. Only if rain is definitely on the cards is it safe to say to your immobilized friend or relative, 'Your garden is looking a bit parched I notice. Do you think I should leave now and give it a spot of water before it gets dark?'

Which brings us to the final entry in this valuable quartet of ideas:

The Old Tom Escape. This gambit is worth a little more than the others, because unlike them it will bear repetition. At the core of the sequence is an imaginary patient on a different floor.

Half way through your visit you can say, 'Well I must go and see old Tom in Ward 27. Sorry, but he'll be devastated if I don't squeeze him in ... all alone in the world ... not much hope you know. ...' Two bonuses of the Old Tom spring to mind: (a) You'll seem golden-hearted and (b) Tom can be available in hospital for as long as your real visitee.

How to Shorten the Stay of Boring Bedside Visitors

Supposing you yourself are in hospital and every day you get a stream of unimaginative, tongue-tied or insensitively garrulous relatives and acquaintances come to blight your bedpanorama of life.

Obviously, a more formidable plan of action is required. It's much harder to get rid of visitors when you're at the prime disadvantage of being unable to move. However, the following ideas have all been tried and not found wanting by some of the more sickly members of the SuperScrooge family.

Presumably you know your visitors well enough to be familiar with their TV preferences. So say something like, 'I'm not sure I expected you this evening with that Paul Newman film on in half an hour's time.' And then to cover yourself: 'At least I heard someone say it was.'

Cousin David's refinement was to quiz his unwelcome visitors, 'Isn't this the night the Dog and Duck are going back to 1958 prices for that publicity stunt thing?'

Another top echelon way of easing an unwanted bedside caller towards the door is to remember who her worst enemy is and to use that name in vain: 'Mary Thompson is coming to see me later on. You know Mary, don't you?' You can see how excuses will soon be made, leaving you in peace again.

It would be crass indeed to try to curtail visits with the bald announcement, 'I've picked up something very contagious while I've been in here.' But the suggestion can be made subliminally. Try your own variations on this: 'There's been a few cases of Whissinger's Syndrome around here. You'll have had it, of course, Aunt Violet. Most people have.'

She knows she's not had it, because she's not even heard of it. She won't admit ignorance by asking about the symptoms. She'll simply fear the worst and buzz off.

The Sting of the Speckled Squirrel

For visitors you particularly dislike may I suggest the Speckled Squirrel. Though fairly new to our repertoire, it's effect is

VISITING TIME

devastating, the only prerequisite being that the victim must have called at your bedside before.

This is how your conversation should go: 'There was an outbreak of Speckled Squirrel Disease in one of the wards last week. I've not heard of it before, but they say it's not at all unknown in hospitals. The consultant was telling us it can be fatal among men of a certain age.'

Your boring visitor will start to fidget.

'A few grey lumps to the complexion are the first signs, apparently. But I can see you're in the clear Uncle Arthur with a marvellous skin like yours.'

On the words 'in the clear' you should hesitate. Stare firmly, but momentarily at Uncle Arthur's face. Look anxious for a second, then brighten up and switch the subject in some haste. Uncle Arthur will depart in similar manner to consult his doctor.

How to Visit Out of Visiting Hours

The inconvenience of hospital visiting times is a mixed blessing. One can always let old Mrs Thompson know you won't be along this week as you're at work when the ward opens to the world. On the other hand, you may be in the first flush of true love and actually *want* to call on your poorly swain. How can you do this at an hour forbidden by the hospital but more acceptable to yourself?

Strongly favoured is a procedure adapted from that used by journalists when they need to interview people confined to bed after train accidents and the like. You should walk into the ward as if you owned the place – wearing a white coat.

Though it will be assumed you're a doctor, this is hardly your fault. Laboratory technicians, electricians, carpenters and people serving in hardware shops are all entitled to wear white.

Prescription for Success

Given the continuing craze to keep fit, it seems odd that queues for prescriptions continue to lengthen in chemists' shops. Is it that pharmacists drag their feet in the hope that hypochondriacs will spot some other remedies on the shelves to buy while they wait? If, like me, you hate kicking your heels in these sniffling queues, because you never know what you're going to catch, you may be interested in the following counters.

You could try transferring your prescription form to a neighbour saying bravely, 'I'm afraid I'm not well enough to go to the chemist's. I'm not fit to be out, you see.'

More ambitious, perhaps, but also more satisfying is the much-lauded Red Form trick. It's performed by sealing your prescription in an envelope. At the chemists you rush breathlessly to the front of the queue, gasping, 'It's a red form case I'm afraid. The patient is parked outside. You'll have to be quick.' As the flustered assistant hurries away you should call out, 'Please hurry.'

In the pharmacy itself, the chemist will make up your very ordinary prescription as a matter of routine. But his assistant, still believing she's co-operated in a life and death drama, will rush the pills back to you. With a hurried 'Might just be in time' you can hurry out the door.

A Faster Service from your Optician

Only politicians outdo opticians when it comes to making promises that aren't kept. How often are you told the new spectacles will be ready on Thursday, only to return on Saturday, and watch while an assistant searches three times among hundreds of sealed envelopes with other names on. Then you're told to come back on Wednesday when the next delivery is due.

It adds credence to the story of a chap who ordered new glasses, then committed robbery on the way home. He was jailed for ten years. On his release he called into the opticians on the remote chance that they still had his new spectacles. 'Ah yes,' says the optician, 'they'll be ready on Tuesday.'

Because of the pseudo-medical feel of an optician's shop – deliberately fostered to excuse high prices – some customers experience a psychological block about making a fuss. But if your glasses aren't ready by the due date, there is a more astute way to make the entire staff feel very small. It was devised by Aunt Carol, who, it was said, took more pleasure in putting people down than in the SuperScrooge Way which, I hope, is to put people right.

Gently remind the optician's staff (the optician himself is usually at another branch making money out of eye-tests) of their duty as guardians of the nation's health. Do this loudly enough for the other customers to overhear.

You took the precaution of putting your present pair of spectacles in your pocket before you came in. So you can now complain to the staff that without your new specs you may fall down a manhole or become victim to an unseen motorbike. Then blunder sadly out of the shop, colliding with a display of frames on the way out.

All the assistants will now feel humbled enough to make sure your specs are delivered personally to your home, probably by the next day.

How *Not* to Do Voluntary Work

All for one, one for all.
> —*Alexandre Dumas, 'Les Trois Mousquetaires'*

All for one
> —*SuperScrooge*

THE key to personal prestige in these caring days is the association one has with unpaid work for national charities or the local community. This is where OBEs and MBEs are won. This is how business and social contacts are made. This is why we're admired and remembered – for our social responsibility and generosity.

A cursory look at *Who's Who* will confirm the number of top people who profess to be Good Samaritans in their spare time. The trouble is, of course, that all this do-gooding can be damned hard work.

And that was the problem for the SuperScrooge movement, and why we put some of our most imaginative minds to it. How to appear to be at the very thick of intense but unpaid activity in the service of humanity, without actually doing a stroke.

It didn't take us long to establish that the basic premise of saving time in the voluntary field is to be associated with it, not committed to it. Everyone must be made to think you're working your heart out, when you're merely snatching the glory.

(The more literate among you might be amused to know that this has become known as The Twist of Two Cities after the Dickensian barrister who took the credit for brilliant defence work while his junior Sidney Carton did all the research. Silly Sid later went on to demonstrate an approach diametrically opposed to that of this guide by laying down his life for another.)

How to Be Appointed to Chair a Meeting

For clarity's sake, let's take a very simple project like organizing a community bonfire for the village on November the Fifth. A notice appears in the church magazine inviting everyone to a preliminary meeting at Tom Johnston's house. Obviously this blighter has designs on chairing the Guy Fawkes Committee.

To secure the job (and the prestige) for yourself you'll need to undermine your rival's position. Even though you've taken the elementary first step of wearing a formal grey suit so that you actually *look* like a chairperson among a sea of woolly jumpers, much more will have to be done. You can, for instance, ask Tom, 'How is your wife now?' The right anxious tone of voice with stress on the 'is' will imply that she needs so much bedside care that Tom won't be able to attend many meetings. Even if he says, 'But there's nothing wrong with Gladys,' this will only be perceived as the brave gesture of a brave man.

Another discrediting ploy is to raise eyes briefly upwards whenever Tom speaks even if the contribution is profoundly sensible. Or, after just a few sentences, 'secretly' glance at your watch to indicate how dull the man is.

I pause here to mention the Accident/Incident technique though it should on no account be brought to bear except by an expert Super-Scrooger steeped in time-saving practice. It's just possible to jostle a rival to the ground, then apologize, but with an action and a subsequent tone of voice which make it appear that the victim himself is to blame. It's one of life's little facts that no one wants to be led by a clumsy clot. (You can see how only extreme skill can guarantee the Accident/Incident doesn't backfire on its proponent.)

For added insurance you should now offer everyone present a bribe: 'It's marvellous of Tom to invite us here today, but for all future meetings there's probably slightly more room at my house.' A number of sound excuses for sliding out of this offer on these future occasions are detailed towards the end of this chapter.

Just about now Tom will announce that he's prepared to shoulder the job of Chairman. But as your various ploys have, by now, thoroughly undermined his position, someone is bound to propose you instead. You will pretend to resist, but the result is inevitable.

Leading a Committee Without Any Real Effort

This first get-together is crucial for the new chairman. He must speak a lot and voice dozens of suggestions. These will be both elaborate and ambitious. They'll take time and effort. The impression begins to form of a committee led by a powerhouse of energy who'll do all this work himself. The meeting breaks up.

On the next occasion (Tom is still the host and has to supply tea and biscuits) the chairman appoints other members to the demanding tasks he's devised for the communal bonfire party. For the complete set of stratagems on how to delegate absolutely everything without being noticed see the chapter on tactics in the workplace.

The way is now clear for the leader to stay away from all other meetings until Bonfire Night when he can reap all the glory for a successful village venture.

It should be added that as a safety measure, a careful team leader will call in at the beginning of at least one meeting to give his excuses. He explains that he's expected to attend an emergency meeting called for the same evening in a nearby big city. 'Sadly,' he regrets, 'this other meeting obviously must have first call on my humble time.'

Note how the larger location and the use of 'obviously they have first call' implies that this second assembly is somehow vital to the whole region.

A useful accessory on these occasions is a simple cardboard file bulked out with junk mail and old Sunday supplements. Blue is the preferred 'important' colour for such a file, preferably secured with rose-coloured ribbon.

A length of pink ribbon is a valuable adjunct to a time-saver's equipment. It's obtained from any barristers' outfitters, but mine originates from the Christmas tree at last year's office party. By now the bonfire committee is feeling grateful that their chairman has found time to call in at all. And his subsequent absences will be put down to this other more vital commitment.

How to Prevent a Meeting Taking Place at Your Home

Once more children prove their value to SuperScroogists, this time in the vital business of cancelling meetings at your home.

Tell your fellow committee members that little Martha has mumps. This is particularly off-putting to men. Normally they can't remember if they had it in infancy or not, but they will recall that catching it in later years can be spectacular.

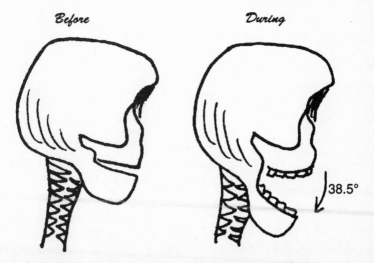

The correct angle to drop the jaw for an effective concerned look.

But note that giving the child a few dabs with lipstick is as old-fashioned as it is unconvincing – just your concerned look will be enough.

An effective 'concerned look' is acquired for this, and countless other dodges, by dropping the lower jaw as far as possible while keeping the mouth closed. This physically causes the mouth to droop. But more than this, for no visible reason, it brings a peculiar expression to the eyes which can only mean, 'The very worst has happened and I urgently need your sympathy and help.'

Those without children should apply the popular stand-by of 'a death in the family'. It's usually thought to be indelicate to ask 'Who?', or in fact 'When?', so this disguised reference to ancient family history needs no elaboration.

Taking Responsibility for Community Tasks Without Doing Them

One of the fundamental constants of Scroogism is that you should only take on voluntary impositions if they can be passed across to your children. This applies particularly to community events, like bonfire parties, charity barn dances, whist drives and so on. Though, of course, if you haven't got any offspring you can always borrow

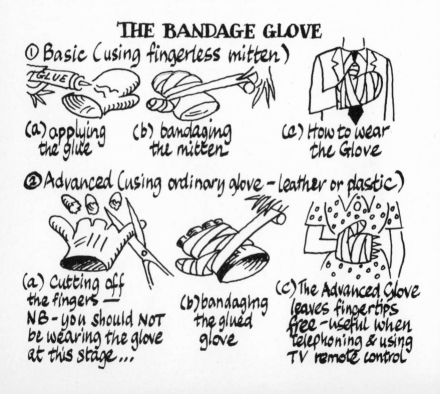

THE BANDAGE GLOVE

① Basic (using fingerless mitten)

(a) applying the glue   (b) bandaging the mitten   (c) How to wear the Glove

② Advanced (using ordinary glove – leather or plastic)

(a) Cutting off the fingers – NB – you should NOT be wearing the glove at this stage...   (b) bandaging the glued glove   (c) The Advanced Glove leaves fingertips free – useful when telephoning & using TV remote control

nephews and nieces 'to entertain' for the evening.

Youngsters can easily collect money, hang up coats, and empty ash-trays. Very much excited by unfamiliar events around them, they'll fail to notice that their parents, so enthusiastic earlier on, are lifting not one finger to help them.

But child-exploitation isn't the only gambit open to the reluctant committee person. SuperScrooge has developed an all-purpose device for escaping earlier obligations at the last minute – the Bandage Glove.

Though I say so myself, no one who seeks to profit by our modest concepts should be without this inexpensive invention. The Bandage Glove, or White Skiver at it's called in Northern counties, is simply made by smearing colourless glue over a mitten. Then a length of household bandage is wrapped around it, and the device is left to set. It can then be used time after time, and at very short notice, to suggest a horrendous injury to the fingers.

Please don't be tempted to use red poster paint, still less ink, to add a little extra drama. Only amateurs relish the unnecessary.

Reaping the Credit for Something You Didn't Do

Let's give an example. You are on the committee of the county's May Ball. Using SuperScrooge tactics you've actually done very little yourself to progress the event. But to consolidate your high standing in the region you need to take all the credit. This is how it's done.

First offer to make a short welcoming speech. Declare that you want to pay tribute to the organizers of the event. This is roughly what that speech should say:

> 'There's no doubt that this ball would not have taken place without the unflagging assistance of Jane Fortescue. She always popped into the right place at just the right time.'
>
> [Note the use of the word 'assistance' which implies that she was second fiddle to yourself. The phrase 'at just the right time' suggests she wasn't actually there very much.]

Your speech continues:

> 'I would also like to thank Rupert Pearce for arranging the printing of tickets.'
>
> [There are three credit-taking ploys in this short sentence. 'I would also like' gives the clear impression that you are top dog. You're in the superior position of being able to give praise for the evening rather than just take it. Then again by thanking Rupert for the tickets and ignoring his many more important tasks you imply that is all he did. And finally if you glance at some piece of paper just before mentioning Rupert's name your audience will believe his contribution was so insignificant that you almost forgot who he was.]

A woman has an extra card to play. She can take the rostrum carrying a bouquet of flowers. This needn't be very large to suggest that fellow committee members have been so grateful for her super-human organizing effort that they've discreetly bestowed a floral tribute just a few minutes earlier.

No one will ask later, 'Who are the flowers from?' as this suggests they're so dozy that they've missed something.

How to Gain Instant Respect

There are numerous positions you can fill in the community which entail a lot of work. Such as town councillor, magistrate or neighbourhood watch organizer. There are however other designations which *sound* as impressive, but which demand less effort, and, more importantly, nobody cares if you miss most meetings.

I include in my list parish councillors. Unlike their counterparts at Town Hall, this group is unburdened by any real responsibility (or indeed criticism) yet they can rightfully append the word 'Councillor' to their names. This is, of course, advantageous when booking hotel space or seeking membership of a golf club.

School governor is another post favoured by time-respecters, and for good reason. It's easy to stay away from meetings because the presiding headteacher doesn't want you there to sour her precious decisions anyway.

But hand in hand with this enviable lack of activity is the sheer prestige of the position. You can be the most ill-educated person ever to walk the high street, but if you're a school governor you walk tall. You're regarded locally as an educationalist and an academic.

Uncle David was a school governor between 1962–79. We all thought him a fine addition to the board at St Edant's, Doncaster, because he was the only member who could see school policy from a child's point of view. Apart from his advanced knowledge of obscure roulette systems and steeplechase handicapping, his educational abilities never advanced beyond the average nine-year-old. But he *was* a school governor and so reaped the benefits of community respect.

For Children's Eyes Only

Oh what a tangled web do parents weave,
When they think their children are naïve.
—Ogden Nash

SPORTINGNESS is, I hope, always the way with Scroogists. So I'm bound to say that it may not be playing the game for any adult follower of our little creed to proceed further with this chapter. You should now pass it across for your children's use only. It will save a lot of your offspring's time and make their relationships with you much easier.

However, as it could do the opposite for your relations with them, perhaps you're inclined to at least peep at the following advice after all. You might just discover some of the tricks they're working on you already. I leave it to your conscience.

Should you take the former course, you can at least redress the balance by studying the next chapter which gives counter-instructions on how to save time in your dealings with younger people.

Incidentally, those without children will still make headway in the art of saving time by studying this section and adapting its contents to adult living. Nevertheless, the chapter is presented in a literary style suitable to junior time-savers.

The Homework Problem

Mums and dads can be pretty sniffy about helping with your homework. They'll say, 'You'll have to learn for yourself, you know.' The real reason is that modern teaching methods left them behind long ago. And they don't want to be shown up. Still, it's always possible to fool them into helping you out.

Dodge One: Parents are scared stiff that teachers will think they have a dim child. For this reason they'll always agree to check your answers. So if you're doing algebra sums, say, simply put down any old numbers. On checking, mum will give you the real answers.

You can pretend to do the sums again and agree with her. It's safer to do one or two sums correctly yourself to avoid suspicion.

121

Dodge Two: If you get high marks for one particular essay, it probably had a proper structure. That means a good start, middle and end. So save this piece of work. Use it as a model for every other one you write. Only a few names, places and other small details will need to be changed.

Few teachers are brainy enough to remember everything you do, so you'll always get away with it. Some famous writers made lots of money doing the same thing.

Dodge Three: The bigger your writing, the longer your essays.

Dodge Four: If you have history or geography questions to answer start a kind of family quiz round the tea table. Casually say, 'I bet nobody here knows the capital of Paraguay,' or 'I know who was made king after Charles II. Does anybody else?' The answers will come flooding in.

Dodge Five: Try sympathy. Tell mum you have a rotten headache. Close work is making it worse. But you'll get into terrible trouble if you don't finish your homework. A few 'tears' from the tap will help. She'll quickly agree to finish your homework 'just this once'.

Ducking Music Practice

Practising a musical instrument is really good because you can do it in a room on your own. Nobody knows what you're up to in there. When I was a schoolboy in the 'fifties, the boom for home tape-recorders was just starting. What I did then, you can try today.

On Monday secretly record your whole practice session. From Tuesday onwards simply play it back. Your family will hear the music through the wall, so any electronic feel to the sound won't be detected. And while the tape plays, you can catch up on the *Beano*.

Naturally you won't be very popular with your music teacher for all your wrong notes at the end of the week. But like all adults speaking to a child, she can be put in a good mood with a joke. Try this musical gag:

Music lover: 'Is your orchestra led by a maestro?'
Musician: 'No we all travel in the same bus.'
(You might have to think about this joke for a bit.)

Otherwise you can practise properly for half the session, record it, and play it back for the second half. This will help to keep your standard up.

How Not to Tidy Up a Bedroom

How often are you told to 'put all your things away nicely' just when you're about to go out. When this next happens to you, put all your

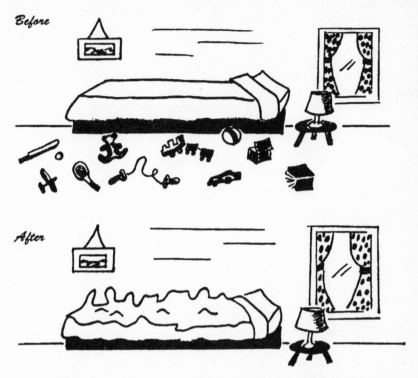

stuff on the bed and cover it with your duvet or bedspread. You can then put things back in drawers when you have time.

Older children will also find it useful to make this little speech to parents (it's important to look quite solemn): 'I think I'm old enough now for you to respect my privacy. That is, if I'm to mature as a responsible person. So would you mind giving me a key for my room so that nobody can come in.' You can then leave as much mess as you like.

Barefooted Cheek

It's a good thing to move about the house in bare feet. This means that any rotten outside jobs which your parents might have in mind, like fetching coal or going to the corner shop, will be dumped on another brother or sister.

Exams Without Really Trying

Teachers aren't supposed to know what's in an important exam paper, but somehow or other it can get out. It says a lot for a teacher's skill if his pupils do well, so there's a great temptation to drop hints in the few days before you sit. So listen carefully. And if you pick up a vague feeling that questions will be asked about a certain subject, make sure you mug it up.

WARNING: THIS DOESN'T ALWAYS WORK.

The bulk of your revision should be done on the night before the exam. Then you won't have time to forget anything.

We all know that it's very important to read exam questions very carefully. But having done that you should start writing very fast as soon as possible. This will throw all other pupils completely off their stride.

Dodging School Games

Given the wide variety of sports now taught in school, this kind of skiving is now a vast subject which we can only scratch the surface of here. The first rule is never be very good at anything. That way you won't have to stay after school to practise for school teams.

If you get a note from your mum and dad asking you to be excused swimming or PT because of a cold, you should show it to the teacher. But try to hang on to it for later use. This is easily done if you ask a classmate to cause a diversion just after the teacher has read your piece of paper. Your friend could, for instance, fall gracefully to the floor in a momentary feint. During this anxious moment the note will be forgotten and you can pocket it.

Nobody pretends this is easy. Timing is crucial. Too early and the teacher won't have a chance to excuse you. Too late and the precious note might disappear into teacher's drawer.

This type of trick is known as a 'double sting' because the pupil who caused the diversion is also excused games. So the next time he has a note you can perform the same service for him.

Running Gags

Cross-country running is one of the worst kinds of torture a school can inflict. This is because, unlike more interesting pursuits, like snooker which is never taught, running doesn't call for any teaching skill. It is, however, open to skiving opportunities.

Sometimes a cross-country course is set out in laps, around a playing field, say.

The idea here is to run to the far side of the course with the group. Hide behind a tree. Idle there until the group comes round again on the last lap, then rejoin it.

It's not advisable to use your rest to storm home to an easy victory, as this might put you in the dreaded school team.

Should the cross-country course take you well out of school grounds, take some small change with you and stroll along until

CROSS-COUNTRY RUNNING:—
How to save energy and come first

your fellows disappear from sight. Then hop on a bus. They'll wonder how you ever got in front.

We Can't All Be a Prefect

Head teachers will often attempt to make promising pupils into prefects. This, they say, is a great honour. Fine – if you want to be an unpaid skivvy. Because this is what they're really after.

So unless you want to blight the 'best days of your life' doing all the jobs a teacher doesn't want to do – or even worse, sneaking on your friends – turn the job down. The correct reply, 'Thank you, but I think my friend John is much the better choice', will make you seem very noble.

And if you're asked to be head boy or girl (a really bum job) say in hurt tones, 'I'm sorry, but I don't hold with favouritism'. Then walk loftily away.

Making the Right School Friends

Brainy types don't make chums with children just because they like them. The following kids are worth getting to know, even if they're quite horrid:

Somebody who lives near you and gets a daily lift to and from school.

An only child whose parents are rolling in it and who like other children to call round to keep him company.

Any pupil whose family has a holiday villa in another country and/or a swimming pool in the garden.

Any pupil with near relatives who run a sweet stall or fast food restaurant.

Any child whom teacher has described in her school report as 'easily led'.

How to Humble a Bully

Blackmail, as they say, is a dirty word. It has no place here. But the related practise of 'having-one-over' (described further in the chapter on business practice) is jolly OK for stopping a bully bashing you up.

As everybody knows, these characters are rotten enough to get up to all sorts of naughtiness as well as bullying. So keep a close eye on your tormentor. Watch if he steals a pencil at the shop or superglues the teacher's desk shut. Then go up to him five minutes later and make some remark which shows you know exactly what happened without actually saying so.

For example: 'Terrible the price of pencils nowadays, isn't it?', or, 'Do they still sell superglue at Woolworth's?'

The bully will turn even whiter if you noted that the stolen pencil was yellow and you then inquire about the cost of yellow pencils.

Frightened that you'll tell somebody, the bully will probably buy you sweets and never bother you again. But if he does, just say 'pencil' or 'superglue'.

Really cheeky kids can use the smashing 'have-one-over' technique on any nasty teacher they happen to spot secreting school paperclips in his briefcase. Or for that matter on mum if she's seen chatting to a strange man in a coffee bar.

Ball Control

You'd like to go to a playground but there's a row of houses in the way. If you don't want to walk all the way round, pitch a ball into one of the back gardens, over the roof if necessary. Knock on the door and ask if you can get it back. Then exit over the rear wall.

How to Escape Punishment

If you're about to be bawled out for your ball's accident with the greenhouse, or any other honest mistake, there's a really good get-out which works with every adult in the land. You'll need some long words, but it's worth it.

You must learn by heart a special way of saying sorry. But instead of saying the usual stuff like, 'sorry' or, 'I was silly' or, 'I won't do it again', try a few long words like 'I'd like to apologize. I was irresponsible and there'll be no re-occurrence.'

Having memorized this speech you say it to the wronged parent or teacher. But be very serious about it and look glum. You will be forgiven straight away.

This is because long words will make you seem grown-up. And adults rarely tell off anybody their own size. They also – and lawyers do very well out of this – believe that long words and being sincere are the same thing.

And Finally

There are two good things about all these dodges. If you do them you'll lead a much easier life. But secondly, your parents and teachers will gradually become very proud of you. They'll begin to see you as a future Cabinet Minister.

Making Children More Useful

Children begin by loving their parents. After a while they judge
them. They never forgive them.

—*Oscar Wilde*

FOR new parents all spare time goes into steep decline the moment
mum goes into hospital. In fact, until they slide into some sort of
routine, which takes forever, both can say goodbye to most of their
leisure. Normally a SuperScrooge publication doesn't pass on un-
complex time and energy savers – like crosswords, there's no fun if
the answers are too simple – but the harrassed plight of desperate
parents screams out for an exception. The following tips come from
S. Jones, consultant paediatrician.

The Very Top Ten Time Savers for Very Young Parents

Don't buy any clothes or toys until the gifts start coming in. Not
only will relatives and friends join in this peculiar rite, but
friends of friends, neighbours and very, very slight acquaintances will contribute too.

Acquire all infant clothes in sizes which are much too big. Babies
adrift in large outfits look cute. If you keep buying garments
which just fit, you'll spend all your time in Mothercare.

Car boots sales are the place for cast-off baby gear. So disposable
is it that the choice here is often better than any specialist shop.

To save time, I'm not giving Mr Jones's seven remaining top
savers, as they're not as good as the tips above.

How Father can Push Feeding Duties onto Mother

The new father should do all possible to ensure baby is breast-fed.
This saves mixing bottles of powdered formula milk at midnight like
a demented sorcerer's apprentice. It also means he stays abed while
mum rises every few hours to do the necessary. And breast-fed
babies are cheaper to run.

Two good arguments he can use here are: (a) human milk gives baby instant immunity to all kinds of nasty infection; and (b) studies show that breast-fed tots are more intelligent. Convincing reasons, aren't they?

Pushing Feeding Duties onto Father

Mothers who want to retaliate for doing all the work can lumber the father with the feeding by trying the breast for a few days (enough to give substantial immunity) before giving in to a terrible soreness. You should be mightily indignant if asked for proof of this.

The Premature Parent

Once the bottle regime is under way, convention dictates that each parent takes turns to stumble around in the night. You can't slide out of this arrangement by pleading a headache every time. What's needed is a more enduring excuse.

In frequent use is the premature heart beat or extrasystole arrhythmia. Though this sounds alarming it's common in normal hearts and nearly always harmless. It can be brought on by a change in normal routine, so is ideally suited as an excuse for people who find themselves jumping in and out of bed at all hours.

What's more, only the sufferer can detect this condition, so nobody can prove you haven't got it, if you say you have. Naturally your loving partner will insist that your nocturnal duties cease until you're better. This, according to Thompson's 'Diseases Without Obvious Symptoms' can take years. . . .

Time Efficient Ways to Stop Crying

Traditional methods to soothe a crying baby – carrying it about, rocking it, singing soppy songs – are useless to an energy conserver of repute. You can't do anything else at the same time. While researching the problem for BBC Radio Four, I came up with these tried and tested alternatives:

Park the infant on a vibrating washing machine, or on the teenage girls next door.

Play a home-made tape of a vacuum-cleaner or food-mixer in action. (This is as good, if not better than those commercial recordings of a mother's womb.)

Play loud music.

Suspend a brightly coloured beach ball on cotton from a drawing pin in the ceiling.

The Sorcerer's Apprentice Syndrome

Around the age of five it's essential that little ones are seriously encouraged to take interest in something which consumes a lot of your time. Examples are weeding, housework or cleaning the car. An early affinity is forged by giving them their own tiny patch of garden or their own special cloth.

Then for the next ten years while you carry out these onerous tasks there's always a happy little soul beavering away beside you.

During the pre-conditioning stage, your diminutive helper should

THE SORCERER'S APPRENTICE
with Forward Projection for 2003 A.D.

be introduced to neighbours with phrases like, 'Here's my indispensable assistant', or, 'Meet the best car washer in the whole of Britain.'
Flattery ensures continuity of service (SuperScrooge maxim No.
3755467X).

You can be more ambitious with an older child. Promoting an
interest in golf supplies a free caddy service. Fostering a preoccupa-
tion with antiques produces a keen silver polisher.

A Devious Way to Get Your Child to Spring Clean

Before we progress, perhaps the position is best made clear. Should
anyone argue how reprehensible it is to trick your own children I
would make two points: (a) The little beggars make a hobby out of
putting one over on parents whenever they can; and (b) They won't
lift a finger around the house otherwise.

Studies show that 87 out of a 100 children shun any activity to
improve the home unless paid in hard cash. The same group of
post-graduates (Doncaster University 1991) discovered that in only
one in 18 cases is it worth setting juniors any kind of chore in a
straightforward fashion because in less than five minutes they'll be
utterly distracted.

Our best counter to this reluctance has its disadvantages (it calls
for expenditure on cakes and buns), but its high success rate secures
redemption.

Invite someone the kids really admire to come to tea. It could be
their favourite teacher, girl-guide leader or the lollipop lady.

Announce the visit a week in advance. Add that you're a bit
worried because you've heard the guest has a home 'like a palace'.
Then add, 'She may be disappointed when she comes here because
our house is like a tip. Perhaps we'd better tell her not to come.'

It will be instantly noticed that your offspring will knuckle down
to scouring, polishing, dusting and vacuuming like never before.
Suggest that the visitor may care to see their bedrooms as well. All
the junk will disappear before your eyes.

And if you toy with plans for tea in the garden, your tribe will
soon be brushing, mowing, weeding and dead-heading too.

A complex Scroogism yes, but a popular one among parents long
exasperated with childish laziness. And for a text-book example of
the gambit in action, I can do no better than refer you to past masters
in my neighbourhood, Bernard and Ruth Thompson.

Just last summer they made it known that a very important
personality indeed was coming round, the striker from the town
football team.

A feverish week-long session of housework and path-weeding was
masterminded and carried out by tiny hands. Then, with just one
day's notice, a typed note came in the post. The star was sorry, but
couldn't come after all.

Bernard swore the personality had intended to honour the invitation. He couldn't tell you how insulted he felt when neighbours hinted he composed the note himself. But it's still whispered to this day that his portable typewriter also has a damaged 'e'.

How to Trick Children into Clearing Up Your Mess

How's this for a prime example of the Art . . . You've managed to get the living-room into disarray with mugs, empty plates, newspapers and magazines. Invite the children to play in the same spot. Then accuse them of making a mess. Insist with a show of temper they clear everything up.

How to Cajole a Reluctant Child into Running an Errand

Allow me now to describe the celebrated Clock Run – a favourite child-besting ploy. So much so that the SuperScrooge Club of New Zealand honoured it with a three-star award at their 1990 Auckland Convention.

Estimate the time it takes to sprint to the corner shop and back. Use this information to make junior a tempting offer: 'If you can run to the shop, buy a bag of potatoes and get back again in four minutes, I'll give you £1.'

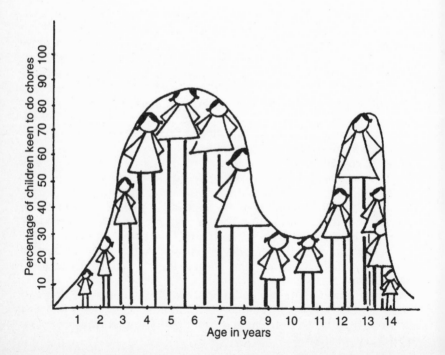

The finely-pitched warm tone and encouraging gesture in the shop's direction will imply that you know this feat can be accomplished very easily and you're simply seeking an excuse to give a little extra pocket money.

Say you'll time the effort by the kitchen clock. Then as junior speeds down the drive move the big band on by one minute.

Once again my critics have pontificated, denouncing the Clock Run as a particularly underhand trick. So it is. And well worth a try.

I understand the New Zealanders have to extend the run's deadline to half an hour because of the distance of 'local' shops.

The Virtue of Hoodwinking Your Children

By this time, there may be a few suspicions invading young minds. But that's no bad thing. Most children admire and aspire to Super-Scrooge methodology. They eventually suss out the various ruses of practising mums and dads, and seek to emulate them. Then a healthy domestic rivalry exists with parents and children seeking to outdo each other. It's a healthy game, certainly more stimulating than chess.

The Instant Way to Win a Child's Permanent Respect

Most parents detect a steady decline in respect from their children as the early teens approach. This could be because: (a) they've not pursued our time-saving philosophies diligently enough to attract youthful admiration; or (b) they've been *too* accomplished and their children haven't detected enough ploys to be able to appreciate them.

Rebuilding parental prestige is an energy-sapping process which could take years. Yet it must be done. Not particularly for the child's sake, but to make him more manageable, more susceptible to parental whim. And, of course, more likely to wash-up, run errands, clean the toilet and so on.

Luckily some instant prestige-building methods are beginning to show results.

One way which combines originality with simplicity, and simultaneously works for two sets of parents, is the Present Swap. Your son John is potty on soccer and wants a football for Christmas. Living next door is James, of a more serious disposition. He asks for a scholarly work on Egyptian ceramics.

In collusion with James's mum, you give John the book, while James receives the football. In both homes there'll be a tearful scene. After a token attempt to persuade your sporting son to accept his learned present, you say, 'OK we'll exchange it for a football', adding, 'In fact, we'll do it right away.'

'How can you?' he wails, 'It's Christmas Day and all the shops are shut.'

You reply (with a conspiratorial wink), 'Where there's a will there's a way.'

You then pop next door to James's home where a similar conversation has taken place. Presents are secretly exchanged. So John suddenly has his soccer ball, James his Egyptian guide and to each set of parents goes the instant and respected status of magicians.

I've used the next door example to simplify the gambit, but as neighbouring children could well meet to compare notes, it's more secure to hatch the plot with parents some streets away.

Another Instant Way To Earn A Child's Respect

Our second suggestion is one of those occasional SuperScrooge tactics which armchair cynics dismiss as tongue-in-cheek. 'Rather clever', they opine, 'but surely never meant to work in practice.' How very wrong!

True, the approach is intricate and certainly requires skill, but its effectiveness knows no bounds. The respect engendered lasts a lifetime possibly living on into family legend.

Imagine the scene. You're walking in a quiet spot with your young family. The wind rises, the light is falling. A rough-looking character approaches. He has tattoos, a Mohican haircut, a sneer and muscles. Lots of muscles. A knife appears, a demand for money.

Do you panic? You do not. The children are gestured backwards. You confront the danger. A chop to the throat, a punch to the stomach, a knee in the ribs. The would-be assailant has gone.

No one says much on the way home – your children are numbed by admiration. You obviously regard your heroism as commonplace. Only later will your magnificent competence as a protective parent begin to sink in.

The only real difficulty is hiring the 'villain' in the first place. A random selection from the street might really get you mugged. A reliable source is a church youth club, where many members look the part while, for altruistic reasons, they'll not overcharge for the service.

In fact, you won't have to pay at all if you spin this tale! 'I've been very ill and I'm not the man/woman I was. But Simon and Jane are only children and don't understand. Unless I can win back their respect with a show of courage I just can't go on. I know I'm asking you to sort of deceive but I'm desperate, desperate. . . .'

You'll have noticed from the above that mothers aren't excluded from this gambit – a female show of force demonstrates their modernity as well as moral strength.

Making your blows convincing is admittedly hard. But you can save the trouble of rehearsal if you merely strike an oriental fighting pose, while snarling 'Harse – ee' or some similar-sounding cry. The 'attacker', now paralysed with fear, hares off without a blow struck. (Well, obviously not quite paralysed.)

It would be dishonest not to report at least one celebrated failure. Cousin Barney had enough common sense to check that no public-spirited person was around to join the attack on his 'ruffian'. But the event backfired when this unfortunate fled into the arms of a policeman previously concealed deep within a shop doorway with a cigarette.

We never discovered if the luckless accomplice ever managed to talk his way out of his dilemma, as, naturally enough Barney removed his young family from the scene without leaving his name.

A New Image – How to Attain One Instantly

> We must set an example – but that doesn't mean we should follow it.
>
> *—Bernard Kops from his play 'Solly Gold'*

NO one must ever accuse us of ordinariness. An adherent of our League must appear alert, active, knowledgeable, well-mannered, gently eccentric in a pleasant British sort of way, wealthy and familiar with all the social graces. I use the word 'appear' because only someone with no respect for time will trouble to acquire all these qualities in the normal prosaic ways. No, the true Scroogist, whether advanced or elementary, will want to be known for these enviable traits almost instantly. Here then, in no particular order, is how.

What's In a Name

Time was when middle and last names were cunningly hyphenated to suggest an ancestral marriage of notables 400 years ago. But from humble beginnings this trick became so common that today anyone with even a genuine double-barrelled name is compelled to use only the last barrel hereafter. And the only way left to us to distinguish a name now is to add a few following initials.

If you put PHD or MD you could be in trouble, especially if there was some material advantage to be gained. But can this apply to initials which don't stand for anything so well known? I think not. But for safety's sake add some initials which apply to your occupation, then you have some justification. . . . Hence Tom Brewster, a long-time member of our Whetwang group and a bookmaker's clerk, adorns his notepaper with 'Tom Brewster BMC.'

In the wake of my name I often add MDC which sounds high up in the military, though I am in point of fact only signifying loyalty to the Metal Detectors' Club. My Uncle Ernest, forever the wag, spoke at many a rotary dinner from 1962–68 under the title Ernest Blower DSL and POIC which, he confided in family get-togethers, denotes Done for Shop-Lifting and Proud Of It, Chummy.

The Newspaper Aid

Another shift of emphasis dictated by changing perceptions is the question of which newspaper to carry. This is a difficult subject to teach. In the 'eighties all my students were advised to carry the Times or perhaps the Daily Telegraph and this still applies today. Even though one only has to look at the audience at a Tory conference to suspect that these newspapers now have some readers of the working class.

Four examples of how correct use of the NEWSPAPER AID can enhance one's image. Spot the SCROOGIST...

Other recommended image-enhancers are the Financial Times or the Economist, both of which suggest affluence and intelligence, without political affiliation, which is useful because many of the best people no longer support the Conservatives.

It is also quite all right to be seen with one of the tabloids as long as you wear top quality clothes (second-hand) and carry a bag from Gucci or Harrods. A popular newspaper carried in this way makes two important statements: (a) You can't be nouveau riche because they only carry 'quality' papers which they don't read; (b) You are in touch with the ordinary things of life which is a trait not of the snobbish but the truly aristocratic.

Wise Scroogists carry a quality *and* a popular paper which shows real breeding. But don't forget to do your bit for the laudable recycling movement by taking your papers from litter baskets at rail stations. Obviously yesterday's paper doesn't matter if you're only carrying it.

The more shrewd among my readers will realize that I have not advised which papers should *never* be carried. Yet I must refute any possible slur that this is because I'm unwilling to upset the proprietors of any publication which may care to file a favourable review.

The Right School

One of the great unfairnesses of life is the way some get a rollicking, but undeserved, start by being enrolled in one of our top schools. But why struggle with bitterness about this inequality. There's no rule I'm aware of that says you can't buy and wear a tie of inadvertently similar design to those of these fine establishments.

And surely one can use expressions like, 'When I was at Rugby' and the like if you ever alighted there by mistake at the railway station. If someone should jump to the wrong conclusion it should hardly reflect on you but upon that foul attitude, snobbery.

House Names – The Choice

For those whose addresses are not quite right for their deserved station, nil desperandum. It's true that the crest on the notepaper is everything but you may still live in the wrong area if you choose the right sort of name for your house. Scroogists hardly ever (willingly) receive visitors – it's not sound economics – so few will know that your chosen name is a mite too grand for the premises. Neither is anyone recommending unnecessary investment in a name-plate.

My first home, 21 Luxor Avenue, a back-to-back in mid-Leeds, became overnight Stacey Towers, suggesting a long ancestral connection with a stately home. Soon I could dispense with the street name altogether as my address, which they considered comic, became well-known among operatives in the local sorting office. This left the fine inscription, 'Stacey Towers, Central Leeds' on my records and correspondence.

Other examples are Howard Hall, Thompson Acres, Bottomley Heights, Waring Gardens and Perkins Pastures. Readers living in marginally rural areas should add the word 'Farm' after existing names.

Further Ways to Seem Prosperous

Once again the potency of Pinner's Word-Play is worth underlining. Take this simple pronouncement on the weather: 'My gardener is always right on these things. If he says on Monday that it will rain, it does. And he's seldom wrong on any other day of the week, either.'

Note just how much information on your high status underlies the obvious in this statement. Not only are you cleverly imparting that you have a servant but also that this employee works full-time. A family retainer in fact – one of the old school who can predict the weather. It also follows that you must have large grounds.

In actual fact the gardener you refer to in your postage-sized back yard is your husband. His forecasts come from the telly like everyone else. But did you say anything more than this?

On different occasions you can use similar terminology to include a cook, handyman, chauffeur, financial consultant *et al*. In some families it is customary to refer to a grandmother as 'nanny'. So, if your child has been parked with your mother for a few hours you can truthfully drop the impressive remark, 'He's with his nanny.'

On a related theme, Cousin Tony, one of our youngest but most promising followers, has two modest possessions which, with careful turn of phrase, give an illusion that he's a landowner of some note. He has a pair of roller-skates and a pond in his small back yard, the latter being an old washing-up bowl lowered into a marigold bed.

Yet he was able to impress a young admirer by telling her, 'I've a bit of a pond on my land. I did some skating on Wednesday night.' A non-sequitur perhaps, but entirely true, though the admirer assumed his pond, described in the deprecating way of the upper classes, was a lake. And she certainly didn't guess the skating was done on the flat patch behind the gas works in Thomas Street.

How to Seem Studious While Never Bothering to Study Anything

Let's first dispose of that nonsense about wearing horn-rimmed spectacles with plain glass lenses. Or bow-ties. Or forced absent-mindedness.

Tony Parkinson leaves this partly finished oil painting (started by someone else) in his front room to suggest his artistic talents. Tony can't draw a straight line.

One has only to look at TV documentaries on scientific subjects to realize that modern boffins appear much more like the rest of us than those 1950s sci-fi films lead us to believe.

No, the real indicator of perceived scholarly achievement lies not in the appearance, but in the props. A copy of Voltaire in French, Homer in Greek and a set of well-thumbed logarithm tables is my personal collection, but a visit to any second-hand bookshop will come with suitable alternatives. Leave them in your briefcase, on your desk, lying around the home.

Being seen with a classical instrument is regarded as 'scholarly', but as these are expensive, I sometimes carry a music stand with me. It's cheap, very light and suggests membership of a symphony orchestra.

Appearing to Be a JNP (Jolly Nice Person) – Part One

Recording all the available ruses on this subject would occupy a volume on their own. But a good grounding is essential if we're to shrug away the unjustifiable slurs of unbecoming conduct so often levelled at the Art. We will therefore offer a few designs to instantly turn a Scroogist into a decent sort.

You're relaxing in a deck-chair when a neighbouring child's ball lands at your feet. Hide it somewhere. When the child calls round to look for his ball, be very sympathetic. Join in the hunt.

Half an hour later with the ball unfound and the infant in tears, worried parents will appear. They will find you still doing your best to search. With difficulty they'll persuade you to desist while their daughter is led home. Some time later call around with the ball, giving the impression you've continued the search.

Whatever your more selfish actions in the future you'll now be known as a cracking good neighbour. The tips on exploiting the folks next door, detailed in the chapter on home life, will become just that bit more effective.

Appearing to Be a JNP – Part Two

That the next device – Inverse Blame Projection – should enjoy the high placing of 24th on our list of 'nice person' plans is due to two factors. It makes a virtue of a disaster which has already happened. And it applies to most locations.

You discover that you left a leaking ball-point on your car front passenger seat. As soon as you can, give a lift to a colleague. Ask him to write down his phone number as you'd like to offer more lifts in the future. Distract him as he writes, possibly calling out, 'Good Grief, look at that lorry!' He finishes writing and puts his pen away. Some time later call attention to ink on the seat and tell him his pen must have leaked.

When he offers to pay for cleaning shrug the incident off and say you'll foot the bill. He'll be very grateful and you can use the same ink blot later on someone he doesn't know.

The above example is specific to me as a leaky pen did the damage, but, with only a little imagination, Inverse Blame Projection can be applied to any previous accident, any victim and any place.

How to Seem Keen on Sport (Primary)

This section and the next are not without significance as they establish your credentials as being fit, active, open-air loving and sharply competitive. Yet nowhere else is Jenkins's Equation, $E = M G$ (energy = material gain), more soundly disproved than in the whole field of sporting activity.

The programme is clear: to leave clues, both verbal and actual, to your sporting life without getting your knees dirty. Here are a few suggestions:

> Buy a cheap squash racket to poke out of a bag to take to work at the same time every week.

> Insert a protruding snorkel in the same bag on a different day.

> Line your pockets with a few golf tees which can 'inadvertently' spill out when you remove your hankie.

> Leave a riding-hat permanently on the hall stand.

Note that all these pastimes, with the possible exception of swimming, are socially acceptable. There's no point in leaving jogging gear, football boots or darts lying about.

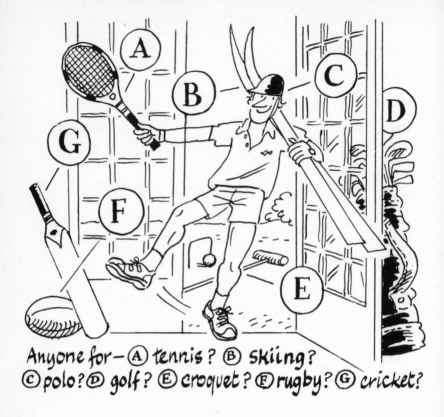

Anyone for— Ⓐ tennis? Ⓑ skiing?
Ⓒ polo? Ⓓ golf? Ⓔ croquet? Ⓕ rugby? Ⓖ cricket?

How to Appear Keen on Sports (Advanced)

A personal favourite makes use of the answering-machine. Record a personal message purporting to be from the manager of a local team: 'Hello, this is Nigel at the Rugby club. Just to confirm that you can manage Thursday again this week. We'll be up against it without you.'

Cousin Barney deserves admiration, if not a bouquet for subtlety, by leaving on his machine: 'Harvey Smith here. I'll call later.' And, as the impersonation is easy, the man exists and no one has cause to doubt the call, why not?

The Celebrity Factor is vital to the sporting image. Young men worried about being thought weak and flabby by young female companions have been known to conspiratorially ask sports personalities at summer fêtes to pass by later on saying, 'Hello, James.'

This kind of gambit doesn't quite make our approved list, as it's hampered by preparation bordering on effort. And it relies on letting someone else in on the dodge which isn't always safe. Waring's Dictate: *Semper attendae posterium* (always watch your back).

More acceptable by far is the 'St Andrews', a device also based on big name association. Supposing you were once watching golf championships at St Andrews. Sandy Lyle was on form. You can now spice your conversation with, 'When I was with Sandy Lyle at St Andrews. . . .' Therefore no lies are told, but there is a misguided assumption by your audience that you play with the best of them.

Pets

I do honour the very flea of his dog.
—*Ben Johnson, 1573–1637*

IF this is a modest chapter then it's because serious time-savers won't countenance keeping a pet, and consequently no one to my knowledge has yet troubled to survey the subject of personal energy conservation in relation to animals. (The Todmorden Study should be discounted as it was made for commercial gain.)

That said, all SuperScroogists admire the cat on two counts: (a) it lives in clover for a third of its life and dozes away the other two; (b) it serves no useful function, yet expects everyone to slave for it.

In contrast dogs do a lot of running around for nothing and, more seriously, wear their owners out. Thus the only breed I can honestly recommend is the greyhound. This may surprise some who don't realize that the fleetest of the canines is as lazy as any sloth. This is why dog races are so short. Apart from the advantage that greyhounds don't *want* to be exercised, there's also little need to do it as there's no excess fat to remove.

Tricking Someone into Walking your Dog

The following extract is from Cousin Barney's well-received 'Neighbours – Only a Doorstep Away'.

Seek out a lonely old soul who lives nearby. Call round one day, your dog in your arms, and say, 'An emergency I'm afraid. The vet says poor old Sammy will have to be put down if he doesn't do a mile a day to strengthen his rear tarsal alignment. He strained it tackling a burglar you know. But I can't manage it today as my Mary is going to the doctor's. [Almost a whisper] She may never run the 400 meters again.'

Author's note: Barney's great-aunt Mary is 96.

In these circumstances. what neighbour could possibly refuse taking the dog for a walk not just then, but probably, if he's any kind of animal lover, every day from now on?

Barney's dissertation also advises, in similar vein, that all new cats should be taken next door and properly introduced to the neighbour's children. This small courtesy will make sure there are always willing hands to do the feeding while you're out enjoying yourself.

It will also stop your pets being persecuted for trespassing next door. It's hard to wing an old boot at those you've been formally presented to, even if they do scratch up the cabbages.

Jumping the Queue at the Vet's

How much more considerate are vets to animals than to their owners? These smug individuals deliberately turn up late to surgery, then leisurely read *Fur and Feather* so that the waiting-room fills up with cats who can then have longer to hiss, claw and generally have fun with budgies, hamsters and other smaller patients. The creatures may have a lively time, but their owners are expected to fret and fester.

But this delay at the vet's can and should be countered. A matchless method of jumping straight into first place in the vet queue was demonstrated to me by a chap who wasn't one of my students but who'd be heartily welcomed if he applied.

There we were, Jeremy the cat and I, at the vet's for thirty-five minutes and still number seven and eight in line for attention. Through the door comes a lanky cross-breed the colour of pale teddybear.

The poor dog's chest and right leg are covered in blood. The distraught owner puts a gory handkerchief to the dog's ear, and more blood drips on the carpet. A forlorn doggy expression adds pathos.

'Cindy was attacked by two Alsations in the park', announces the owner to the queue in general. 'Please, please let her go in first.'

How could we refuse? Well quite easily, thank you, if we'd known the real facts. These weren't discovered until another twenty minutes later when I anxiously asked the vet how Cindy was. A blank look held the clue.

Cindy had only come in for an anti-worm injection. Her owner is an artist who'd apologized for spilling crimson lake over her. There was obviously more poster paint in the hanky he pressed to her ear.

One has to respect the expertise of this ployster. A lesser

practitioner of the 'Art' would have used more easily obtained tomato ketchup without pausing to consider the give-away smell. Or he might have employed ordinary paint rather than the more realistic darkness of crimson lake.

For those doubters – I acknowledge their existence – who dismiss this as a shaggy dog story, I can only say that not only did it happen, but I've friends who've profited from this fine ruse ever since.

Dogs – Earning their Keep

The most prolific professional mongrel I know accompanies buskers on the London Underground system. As black as poverty, collie-like and soulful of eye, he features at 17 stations on both the Northern and Victoria lines, always with a different master or mistress for the day.

This admirable animal has several telling postures to suggest hypothermia, hunger and deep misery. Yet it still manages to convey that the busker is a caring animal-lover who'd give his last few pence to buy a tin of Lassie.

If ever there was a chance that doggy students would pay their fees I would enrol this busker's assistant as a teacher at one of our colleges tomorrow.

Alas most domestic dogs are too lazy and untalented for almost any kind of task. But some, especially labradors and springer spaniels are bred to fetch, so it's not hard to train them to pop along to the newsagents for your Sunday newspaper.

Begin by giving a few biscuits to the shopkeeper to offer your dog just before he inserts the paper in its mouth. Soon your best friend will be so eager to reach the newsagents he won't bother to take you. It's only a short step from there to send the dog with a shopping-bag and a list inside for more ambitious errands. And the shopkeeper will become so amused at this, he'll soon supply his own biscuits.

The Advantages of Cat Ownership – Without the Cat

Cats are unemployable. All they really do is provide furry comfort and stave off loneliness. Some say that if you stroke a cat it provides more relief from all sorts of complaints than you can expect from your GP. Which doesn't, on reflection, seem to be saying much.

It appears to me, however, that a large fluffy toy in the shape of a cat, bunny, badger or vampire bat will serve the same purpose. Just sit it in the same chair by the fire every night and fondle it from time to time.

You can even buy a life-sized paper cat to stick in the front window to welcome you home. Though SuperScroogists have too much of a hold on reality to need such an illusion, this gimmick does serve some purpose in fostering the impression among neighbours that you're an animal lover and therefore a good egg.

Family Events –
Numbing the Pain

It is a melancholy truth that even great men have poor relations.
—*Charles Dickens*

BY social events we mean all those ominous islands on the calendar which leach extra effort from our already overcrowded year, Christmas, Easter, Bank Holidays, Mothering Sunday *et al*. All these customs would be enjoyable were it not for the undignified last minute charge-around that precedes them.

Much useful ground in saving money on the festival circus was covered in the first SuperScrooge manual and, though principles of frugalism often overlap those of time-conservancy, there's no plan to repeat those earlier notes here. However, as SuperScroogism is an infant science, many novel ideas on higher forms of effort-preservation have been evolved recently. The cream of this research is collated here.

CHRISTMAS

On the Cards

A moral stand is always a useful device and one can be taken on Christmas cards. You can put it around that you're not sending many from now on as they can:

1. Commercialise a sacred event.

2. Destroy trees.

3. Pollute the atmosphere with petrol fumes in the delivery.

4. Exploit child labour in third world countries.

Instead, you say quietly, a donation will go to your favourite charity. After all no rules exist that the exact amount you would save on cards must go to your preferred good cause which is probably yourself anyway.

There is also the lost-in-the-post excuse which can be brought to bear for any one of your former recipients who don't know each other.

My own theory is that so many people claim cheques, letters and bills fail to arrive for their own nefarious reasons that the Post Office is unjustifiably pillaried (sic). The only item I can recall ever disappearing en route was a slightly less than appalling school report. And even then one hazily remembers altering one's address in the class register.

Initiates of Scroogecraft also learn how to register the right tone of voice to make the sending of cards to colleagues and business contacts seem somehow to be in questionable taste. (It's hard to describe a tone on the printed page, but it's instantly recognizable on the hearing.)

The procedure is to send no one in your office a card but to employ the 'tone' when thanking them for their's. This way you won't seem meaner than they, but just a shade more sensitive to etiquette.

Saving Time on Christmas Decorations

Encouraging neighbouring children to make decorations may save buying them, but how do you make the lazy blighters do it? Unusually I found our network of study groups rather slow to find any novel solutions to this poser, so I fall back on my ploy, at least ten years old. I offer a penny a link for paper chains, which sounds a lot to youngsters, but actually only amounts to £1 for 25 feet.

If you don't mention paper and glue in the verbal agreement, you can remind your contractors later that they're legally bound to supply these at their own cost. But as this bombshell could unleash that kind of messy reprisal which involves scissors and your loose covers, it's not recommended. Instead I take the generous course by supplying old paper bags in dusty shades of green and red. They may not be as brightly coloured as special festive paper, but the muted pastel effect is more tasteful I think.

Tree-Craft and Other Ways of Saving Christmas Time

A real fir used to be de rigeur, but, thanks to the green movement, artificial ones are in again. This not only saves time buying a tree every year but Uncle Ian has evolved a decorating technique which has since spread through the Movement like wildfire.

He ties on all the baubles firmly, glues on the tinsel and crackers, secures the fairy lights with rubber bands and lashes the fairy on the top.

On Twelfth Night the whole glittering edifice disappears into the loft covered with a large polythene bag ready for next year. The saving on unpacking, putting on, pulling off and repacking is 3 hours 12 minutes.

Uncle Ian's neighbour Douglas also introduced a masterful Christmas concept which isn't diminished by being his only publishable contribution to SuperScrooge philosophy. (Other stratagems were submitted but our lawyers were unhappy.)

In 1982 he obeyed tradition by placing in his living room a bowl of mixed nuts. As he failed to provide nut-crackers, this generous selection didn't diminish. And the very same brazils, walnuts and almonds, their powdery decay invisible under the shells, have been displayed, *sans* crackers, every year since.

The Importance of Keeping Santa Alive

The belief in Father Christmas should be nurtured for as long as possible. This is because of his convenience as a butt of complaint for supplying rather shoddy toys. And for not bringing what he was asked for, especially if it's on the pricey side.

Passing responsibility for a disappointing Christmas isn't only useful for parents, but aunts and uncles can also explain to a tearful infant that the matching scarf and mittens weren't at all what they stipulated in the letter to Lapland – 'I can only think that the Snowy Grotto must be short of bicycles this year.'

Then One Foggy Christmas Eve

Students who train with us already appreciate the 94 recorded benefits of spending, in the interests of economy, all twelve days of Christmas not at your own home but by the hearth of different friends and relatives. But as these papers put the emphasis on energy-hoarding, a few notes on how to slide out of promises to visit particularly irksome relatives must be included.

Your best ally here is the weather. Relations, especially older ones, worry about your welfare. So if you claim there's black ice on the road, you won't be expected to travel. Unfortunately this excuse isn't as potent as it might be as TV weather forecasters can give the game away by divulging 'mild conditions all over the country'.

However fog is a different matter. It can occur in both tepid and freezing winters, and is often localized. So if you have a trip of just two miles to make you can confidently claim a real pea-souper at your end, while your expected destination basks in winter sunshine.

As usual a bit of forethought can make this sort of excuse even more convincing. Just mention around June that you hope the mists won't be as bad this winter as you live in a 'bit of a dip'/near a river/ between two hills/ not in a smokeless zone. No one will run a check that none of these conditions is entirely accurate.

Ideal location for 'fog-prone' home.

The Easter Solution

Choosing Easter eggs takes longer here than anywhere else in Europe for the paradoxical reasons that all British versions look alike. It's a real chore to try to find something a bit different. You won't come across many that aren't the same size, covered in purple foil (oddly the colour of death) with garish boxes depicting unprepossessing TV cartoon animals.

As Easter eggs are never solid and are 'packed' with a few sweets in a minuscule bag rattling around inside, one wonders why they cost so dear. The answer I unashamedly have it from a confectioner is that 'Easter products are all packaging.'

Here lies the clue to getting out of buying chocolate eggs. Explain to your children that all that cardboard comes from chopping down trees in warm countries.

'And you know your cuddly monkey upstairs. Well he has lots of cousins who live in those warm forests. And if we buy a lot of chocolate eggs, cuddly monkey's cousins will have nowhere to live. And they'll all get cold. And they'll die. Now do you *really* think we should have Easter eggs this year?'

(Even fervent admirers have occasionally derided me for applying moral blackmail on minors. But surely it isn't that. In the vernacular of the admirable films of James Cagney, 'I prefer to call it persuasion.')

A varied selection of British eggs.

Bank Holidays – Pain-Easement

Cancelling out the bonus of an extra day off is the threat of a visit from friends you've grown out of, or from free-loading relatives. The bank holiday is even more likely to bring an unwanted carload down upon you if you've moved recently. They now have the excuse of 'dying to see your new house'.

Your advantage and their handicap is that they've never been before. So you can post them a home-made map. During the war, just one tiny slip in the draughtmanship, if made early on, sent many a

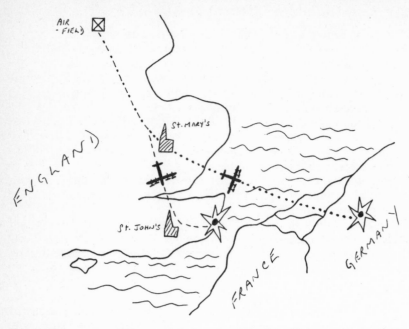

Sketch shown to court martial showing Fingle's bloomer. Just a tiny navigational mistake results in war-time tragedy.

bomber miles off course. The same principle – Navigator's Block – is available to you now.

The unwanted bank-holiday visit is just one of the many reasons why seasoned SuperScrooges have detachable name plates on their country mansions which they can rapidly unhook in an emergency. A few have even re-named their homes after others in the same village to further confuse and delay those who come calling.

Marginally more valuable as a gambit because it's harder to blame the blunder on you afterwards is to relay directions over the phone. Simply miss out one instruction like 'turn left at the lights' and the raiding party will arrive very late, if at all.

If, on the other hand, you're bound to pay annual duty visits, perhaps to those who may favour you in their will, a bank holiday is as good a time as any. As it's that kind of special occasion when you're likely to be in heavy social demand, you can pay up to four different calls on the same day, thus paring down visiting time, without giving offence.

Also, social scientists agree that house calls made on a bank holiday are better recalled by a ratio of 2:1 over ordinary weekends and 3:1 more than weekdays. Which means you'll appear to be a more regular visitor than you actually are (Support for the Bank Holiday Remembrance Theory: the Thompson Report 1989).

Mother's Day – With Particular Reference to Florist Manipulation

As this nuisance, manufactured by a greedy retail trade, befalls everybody at the same time, and all mothers like, or at least get, the same sort of thing (anything smelly, i.e. flowers, soap, toilet water), you can lean on a colleague to buy the very item for your mother that he buys for his.

If you forget to send a card in time (28 per cent of sons and a fifth of daughters according to the Barry Island Census, 1989) you should ring up the florist nearest to her and give him a sob story.

'The aircraft carrier was delayed by a typhoon in Hong Kong. I've got these daffodils, but I won't make it in time to my old mum now. She'll be very upset. I know it's late, sir, but can you deliver her some flowers tonight and I'll make it up to you?'

As people always get a bit sloppy over other people's mums, especially when their sons risk life and limb in the armed forces, not only will a bouquet be rushed round in your name, but charges might be waived as well. And as you never actually said you were on this delayed vessel or in the Royal Navy at all, your honesty, so sacrosanct to a SuperScroogist, stays intact.

There are two extra subtleties in the above telephone call to the florist you may not have spotted.

Addressing him as 'sir' adds conviction to the story as only service personnel do this nowadays – out of habit.

Also note the careful use of 'daffodils'. The florist, bursting with professional pride may well think, 'I can do better than daffodils for this brave lad' and the bouquet he delivers may be quite splendid.

How to Forget Someone's Birthday

There's little by way of defence against other people's birthdays not described in the earlier SuperScrooge manual, other than to forget them altogether. Some approved excuses afterwards are (a) 'The computer let me down,' or (b) 'I had a touch of jaundice, hardly noticeable really, but it's not done the old memory any favours.'

As for one's own birthday, it's best not to mention it. You're not likely to get one extra present. And who really needs a card from colleagues, perhaps with an embarrassing rendition of 'Happy Birthday to You' and, horrors, a round of drinks you may end up paying for!

How to Speed from a Party Early Without Causing Offence

Though parties are a jolly good thing because there's no entry fee and you can meet a lot of exploitable contacts, there are inevitably some get-togethers, usually of a formal or family nature, where you'd rather not be. Fortunately, thanks to support from our socio-psychology department, we can pass on a way to impress upon hostesses that you've been present all evening while actually staying for only half an hour.

Turn up early. This implies that you couldn't wait to come. Whiz round conversing with as many guests as you can, while lingering only a few minutes with each. Try to say something they'll remember. Blatant flattery like, 'I really like your dress. Gucci, isn't it?' or, 'haven't I seen you on TV?' is best. It also helps to wear something conspicuous, like a low-cut dress or a pink bow-tie. Then slope off without saying goodbye.

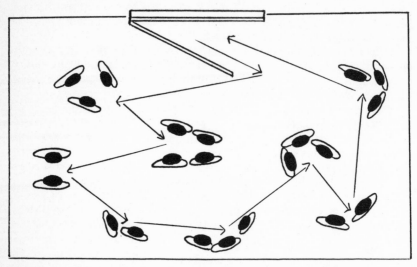

How to speed from a party early.

The hostess will hazily recall seeing you chat to nearly all the guests at some time or other, falsely concluding that you must have been around for hours.

This sleight of feet illusion is a boom to those negotiating the Christmas Party Hop, trying to visit all three functions held on the Friday night before December 25th.

The Weekend Party

Never speak disrespectfully of Society. Only people who can't enter it do that.

—*Oscar Wilde*

AT this stage of my modest tutorials you'll be well on the way to being comfortably-off (only the poor use the word 'rich') with plenty of newly-found time to lounge around at will. But if you want to carry the momentum to the peak and savour the glorious inertia of high society, you'll need guidance on how to make the most of that happy institution – the weekend house party.

Though this high echelon form of entertainment isn't exactly back in vogue, it is nonetheless enjoying a quiet revival, due no doubt to the continuing dearth of imaginative television, and the groundless trumpeting of politicians that we've seen the last of our beloved class system.

The following pointers, aimed at high-flying Scroogists who aspire to weekending in country mansions, are also adaptable for primary students of the Art who wish to cut their teeth in friends' cottages.

How to Be Invited

I needn't recall that it's bad form to fish for invitations to weekend at country mansions, but even unfinished SuperScroogists will eventually attract enough attention to be sought out for invitation, as nowadays 'quality' is hard to find.

Uncle Cecil, of whom it is sometimes said, not unfairly, that he's too confident for his own good, did, in fact, contrive to attract offers in a way which should never be contemplated other than by true experts in our field.

He would scan gossip columns of the Mail, Express and Tatler for news of a weekend gathering of note. Then he'd enter a prestigious hotel to write to the hostess on its crested notepaper: 'I'm in your country again for a meeting in the city on Monday. But I could just about make it a few days early for the bash with Lord Demclock and the Countess if you wish. Regards, Omar.'

Knowing that the only Omar likely to be known to the country home-owners is Omar Sharif, Uncle Cec reckoned the odds at seven to four that, though they probably don't know the film star personally, they'd be intrigued enough to wing a last-minute invitation to the hotel. All he needed to do was to pay a call to the reception desk to claim the letter.

Naturally it took a great deal of cool courage to survive the ensuing weekend as mournful Uncle Cecil looks more like Lassie than any other film star, and hasn't even seen *Doctor Zhivago*. But his studiously acquired social graces (see chapter on Image) and his attractive buoyancy in the face of dreary fellow guests sees him through.

CORRECT METHOD OF ARRIVAL FOR COUNTRY WEEKEND
A—single ticket from Paddington B—battered pre-war leather suitcase with trans-Atlantic liner labels C—checked cap, tweed D—Barbour E—"WEEKEND GAM" (polo injury) F—baggy cords

It should in fairness be recorded that Uncle Cec did some time ago adopt the middle name of Omar. This was after taking a shine to Sharif's character who despatched a stranger for drinking his water in *Lawrence of Arabia*.

The Correct Method of Arrival

Even if you have a Rolls Royce, the correct way to descend on a country house is by train. As per tradition it helps if the old-fashioned platform is bedecked with geranium pots. Carry in your hand a vintage leather suitcase. All these familiar trappings will help to stir in your hostess that Victorian sense of hospitality which is more bountiful than its modern counterpart. Example: She may well bring out the old-style port glasses which hold more.

Unlike those old Sherlock Holmes films, there'll be no ageing cabby available, so the hostess will have to send her car. The benefit of this is not primarily saving money but appearing a shade more important in the eyes of fellow guests (visitor is not a word used in the best circles).

Buy only a single ticket as another returning guest may offer you a lift back on Sunday night.

First Impressions

Begin the popular 'Weekend Gam' (a painful-looking hobble) the second you leave the carriage. If you forget you can hardly introduce it later on and still have your 'old wound' or, if you're young, polo injury, accepted as a plausible excuse for demurring long walks, tennis, ping-pong and other ordeals.

If you have poor sustainable concentration it's perhaps wiser to dispense with the Gam. You'll need to employ it continuously for 27 waking hours. Just one slip, changing your right leg to your left, say, will be calamitous.

The only known get-out, and goodness, isn't it weak, is to tell anyone who may have spotted your goof that you've always believed in Doctor Pilkington's Way: 'This cove says you can ease the pain of one injury by imagining you have another, just as painful, in a different part of the body. Can't see it, myself. Just thought I'd give it a go.'

Actually there's some truth in the theory. The next time you have toothache imagine it in another molar on the far side. The pain will ease.

You must quickly voice this excuse if there's any danger, however slight, that anyone may have seen your bungle. Don't wait for someone to remark on it because weekend guests who're British, never will. To your face, that is.

What to Bring

Fortunately a bottle of wine or flowers should not be pressed on the hostess on arrival. This is an insult, an unwitting attempt to subvert hospitality with payment. (In his excellent *Etiquette for Frugalists*, Tony Brown says this rule strictly applies in all circumstances, however humble the function. As Tony has only thrown one party in his life when he reached the age of forty he felt justified in marking a unique occasion by lifting the rule *pro tem*. And, forgiving a shortage of sausage-rolls, a very fine bring-a-bottle-party it was.)

Also not done is to bring your own towels, soap or hot water bottles. But you could pretend to be very old-fashioned and leave boots for cleaning outside your bedroom door.

How to Have an Easy Time of it

A stay in a country house is a fine opportunity to test the merits of Edwards's Equation which, if successful, and it usually is, you'll want to repeat in all sorts of situations. J. Edwards, who was a noted headmaster before three years mysteriously disappeared from his curriculum vitae, was to state, 'An initial burst of force equals two days of rest.'

You can turn this truism to advantage by taking the lead in any preparations for the weekend. You should draw up a timetable of sports and activity, erect the card table, chop firewood, wash-up and draw the curtains on Friday evening. You must do all this quickly with energy and efficiency.

Then, having established credentials as a bundle of helpful crack-a-jack energy and a thoroughly good sort, you can get away with not doing another thing until departure on Sunday afternoon.

An Excuse to Oversleep (Routine of the Battered Clock)

One annoyance, probably the chief one, about the weekend party is being expected to rise at the early hours of 9:30 on Saturday and 10 o'clock on Sunday. To counteract this difficulty I always bring a very large, very ancient, tin alarm-clock. As this is never set it never goes off. Which is why I can finally appear just before lunch, clutching my clock and loudly swearing never to trust it again.

Appearing to be a Thoroughly Nice Weekend Guest

The key to this is the hostess's children. You must not only learn their names, but also their birthdays. Some small researches, perhaps in the Times cuttings library if the family is of the right stock, will provide the information.

Thus armed, one of your first tasks 'on weekend' is to fleetingly ignore any guests who may have arrived before you, and begin by gushing over the children, 'Why it's little Robin, and what about your birthday? I mustn't forget that must I and it's only 16 weeks and four days away.'

You can see how this sort of thing will go down well with admiring parents. And having established yourself as affable and avuncular at the beginning of the occasion you can now afford to relax into the combination of selfishness and inconsideration which may be your true self. Though I hope not.

How to Be a Maestro and Still Play Wrong Notes

As no real country pile is without its product of Steinway and Sons this is a fine opportunity to show off talents at the piano. The trouble is that without daily practice – and who would want to waste time on that – any kind of classical recitation is beyond most of us.

Yet on these occasions only serious music will do. It *is* just possible to perform *Knees Up Mother Brown* and the like, but only as a joke interlude between the Rachmaninov and Chopin. But don't let all this put you off a short evening performance which may, after all, help you to be reinvited again and again.

Every pianist whose aspirations never progressed beyond a year's childhood purgatory in the front room should not be without an easy-to-play version of the classics. Cut out the simplest piece in there, without sharps or flats, and paste the pages into a difficult-looking score, perhaps salvaged from a car boot sale.

Play through this piece a few times only, picking out the tune and more or less ignoring the troublesome left-hand part.

Soon after arrival on Friday secrete your doctored music in the host's piano seat among all the other ancient manuscripts bound to be in there. Actually it doesn't matter if it's empty. Piano seats are only opened on average once every five years (see *Chippendale's Furniture Manual, 1786*).

At an appropriate time – immediately after dinner on Saturday is recommended (certainly not later as drink impairs performance) – let it be known in a roundabout way that you can tinkle the ivories.

Uncle Ernest's opening line is worth emulating. After earlier noting the date inscribed on the grand piano he would say excitedly, 'I do believe that's an 1886 Steinway. I haven't played one since Harrow.' This always amused us because though we didn't know for sure which make of instrument graced the assembly hall at Harrow Secondary Modern in 1949–53, we've good evidence that it was later sacrificed to a piano-smashing competition at the Durham Miners' Gala.

The Performance

Once everyone knows you can play, you'll be prevailed upon, as a defence against flagging conversation, to oblige. It's not safe at this stage to say, 'I'll do my best, but I'm a little out of practice.' This, in the understated codes of country house parlance, means, 'I'm bloody good.' No, it's far wiser to fumble around in your pockets for spectacles you can't find. Then no one will expect very much.

While reaching into the piano stool you should say, 'I don't play by ear I'm afraid.' This is said in a tone which relegates memorized piano-playing to the vulgarity of the tap room. Now produce from the stool your score with the easy piece inserted inside.

Then play it, making liberal use of the sustaining pedal which obscures any dropped notes and disguises wrong ones. Carry on playing with artistic concentration, whatever starts to go wrong. If you should strike a very obvious bum note, hold it on for longer than written while gazing upwards at some kind of vision only you can see.

A lesser authority on hiding inept musicianship (Thomas Brown, *The Reluctant Past Artiste*, 1983) holds that audience attention to a sequence of wrong notes can be averted by smiling at the moment of disaster. This is based on the premise that normally a player will only relax to acknowledge the listeners at a point when the performance is going to plan.

Both techniques have proved effective, yes, even at Carnegie Hall, but mine, I think, has the advantage – it actually adds to the exponent's aura as a sensitive musician.

Always in your favour is that classical music is runner-up in the list of subjects which people falsely claim to know something about, wine taking first prize. Jenkins's well-known survey shows that though two in five claim a strong knowledge of serious music, only 0.3 per cent of these can spot a wrong note in Tchaikovsky's first piano concerto and 12 per cent thought Rossini wrote his famous theme specially for the Lone Ranger.

But if, after your flawed performance, a fellow guest looks shocked, quickly explain that you hope nobody minded but you were using diminished sevenths instead of minor thirds as 'a bit of an experiment'.

Let's All Go Down to the Pub (A Warning)

Should you find yourself at a rather inferior weekend party you may hear some menace suggest you all abandon domestic cosiness for a more lively evening at the village hostelry. This is often the party-giver talking and marks a classic case of Stingy Host Syndrome: protection of the drinks cupboard against further onslaught.

To acquiesce is to invite double trouble. First, you'll have to pay for a round, perhaps two or three, at today's prices, when the final aim of all 'weekending' is to avoid any expense whatsoever. Second, you'll be expected to make small talk, really small talk, to retired agricultural labourers with cloth caps and cloth ears who are optimistically described as 'characters'.

Alas, you're not likely to make much progress with, 'But I'm really enjoying the truly traditional hospitality here at the hall. Let's not spoil it with all that chemical muck they call beer down at the Spotted Duck . . .', especially if the conversation began a slow death well before dinner.

Until recently the only recourse in my files to control this unwanted development was to bow out of the village expedition by pretending that the pub's smoky fug will bring on the old asthma, then to sweat it out with the host's brandy and cigars until they all wander back.

But the problem deserves a stronger approach and, after some not very strenuous application by a few of my senior consultants, we found it. Simplicity itself. Merely say that your favourite uncle, 'the only father I've ever had really', is having emergency surgery tonight and you'd like to be in to take the call.

The Parting

There are just three rules of interest to the Scroogist who's had an easy time and seeks re-invitation:

(a) You're not leaving a hotel so it's not required to tip servants.

(b) Check you've not accidentally left a lurid paperback by your bedside but that you have purposely abandoned a copy of a play in Ancient Greek.

(c) That you make a big thing of saying goodbye to the children.

Appendix I

How to Waste the Time of People you Don't Like

By way of amusement, and yes, a relief from the relentless study required by the book proper I offer now, at the publisher's suggestion, a list of ploys to waste the time of those who've ever snubbed us, humiliated us, let us down or have faces one can't really like. While I would never dream of hinting that any SuperScroogist lacks courage, most of these little ploys have the advantage of anonymity.

Put through several phone calls to the victim at differing times of the day. In several disguised tones ask if Rupert is there. Make your last call at midnight. Then at three a.m. ring up to ask chirpily, 'Rupert here! Are there any messages?'

If expecting a call from an undesirable leave this message on your answering-machine: 'I'm unable to take your call at the moment. Meanwhile here is some music.' An appalling dirge you recorded earlier can now be played. It may be some time before the victim realizes she's paying for this fruitless call.

You've had a parking ticket which you think is unjust. The yellow lines were beaten away by the weather, say, or you were delivering some clothes to a charity shop. Wait for the reminder then write to the department concerned with a pedantic query i.e. Did this happen on a Wednesday or a Thursday? When they reply wait a fortnight, then ask, 'Are you sure the traffic warden noted the right car?' Continue this steady correspondence until some frustrated official 'accidentally' loses the paperwork.

The Bottom Line

A useful retaliation against those social miscreants, the obnoxious mother with a tiresome baby, has been referred to by chroniclers before this one as Elderman's Soggy Bottom, reputedly after the Newcastle scoutmaster who employs it. The manoeuvre is particularly satisfactory against the kind of parent who arrives at a party with its uninvited infant, so hogging all the attention from the coochi-coo brigade.

The opening move involves a trip to the kitchen to rinse your hands. Don't dry them. But return to pick up the toddler in what appears to be a gushing demonstration of unbridled admiration. After this show of affection the baby, who was supported by your hand, will now have a moist behind.

In this over-hygienic age, the modern parent always regards a wet baby as a public disgrace – so mum will rush off to the bathroom to change its nappy. There's a good chance this will be entirely un-necessary . . . but if it *was* you can always try again – say, every half hour.

Appendix II

Common Wastes of Time

1. Electric knives, automatic tin-openers and toasted sandwich makers.

2. Complaining to trade associations whose *real* job is to protect their members against customer complaints.

3. Many of the tedious preparation techniques illustrated in DIY manuals.

4. Checking old pennies to see if any are valuable.

5. Counting to see if there really are 3000 ideas in this book.

6. Asking 'When *did* you call?' of someone who begins a telephone conversation, 'Where have you been? I've been trying to reach you all day.' (They haven't at all.)

7. Sending for a china mug offered by a commercial firm. There's always a thumping great advert on the side of the mug not shown in the advertising blurb.

8. Trying to get your 'very pretty' baby accepted as an advertising model.

Appendix III

As we were going to press our East Anglia group, dependable, yet often over-deliberate, submitted a few late additions. We've only had time to include a few in this current record of the Art.

The Stammer Factor

This device is useful for attempting to continue a telephone conversation with a self-important individual who shows urgent signs of wanting to hang up on you. A solicitor, say, or the managing-director of a firm you wish to complain about.

You should suddenly assume a speech impediment, making it difficult to spit words out. Only a person with no human feelings whatsoever will interrupt a stutterer when he sticks between words. The conversation will continue as long as you want it to.

The Look

This is a useful adjunct to the repertoire, usually as a convenient device to prize more effort from someone currently under exploitation than they might otherwise want to give. Simply pause in front of the subject and gaze expressionlessly into her eyes. This will induce a vague feeling of unexplainable guilt, encouraging greater speed and diligence.

Our East Anglian party are eager to stress that this look must be held for 1.3 seconds only, and there should be no narrowing of eyes or other too-obvious signs of impatience. This mars the effect which is essentially one of understatement.

Issuing an Invitation You Don't Want to Be Taken Up

Happily, the world bursts with people anxious to entertain us for the evening, usually to a more ambitious meal than we would pay for in a restaurant. The drawback – and it's considerable – is that one's expected to reciprocate.

The solution is to send a picture postcard of somewhere remote (you don't actually have to live there) saying, 'Thanks for the lovely evening. We're rather poor at issuing formal invitations. But please *do* drop in next time you're passing.' You won't be pestered for two reasons: (a) Nobody ever calls unannounced nowadays and (b) the odds are they won't chance by this part of the world for a long time (if ever) and by that time you'll have 'moved'.

Musicanship

A gloriously effortless device this for establishing fraudulent credentials as a person of culture. Merely leave a written score of some complexity, by Brahms or Schubert perhaps, on the music stand of the piano. It's better if it's in a difficult key with lots of sharps or flats. This piece of music should be propped up in a permanent position, ideally with a pile of similar compositions on the piano top. Cousin Tony used to augment the ploy by leaving a blank score by the piano with a few notes inked in, as though he was beginning a symphony of his own.

Tony Parkinson's unfinished symphony.

Getting Instant Action from your MP

Supposing you want to put pressure on the Environment Department not to send a three-lane motorway within two yards of your front door. You go along to your MP's Saturday morning surgery where he promises to object on your behalf. But you know he's given a contrary assurance to the local contractor who's building the road. So what can you do?

Blackmail is too blunt a weapon and deserves to be excluded from our code. But there's no harm in saying in jokey fashion as you move towards the door, 'And you'd better support me in this or I'll tell your wife what you've been up to in London, you old rogue.'

MPs being MPs, there's a good chance that you'll hit a raw nerve. Your member may well believe you know something embarrassing about his private life: a skeleton in the London cupboard somewhere.

Conclusion

The reasonable man adapts himself to the world; the unreasonable one persists in trying to adapt the world to himself. Therefore all progress depends on the unreasonable man.

—*G. Bernard Shaw*

ALL twenty-six study groups who helped to evolve the finer techniques of SuperScrooge 2 are facing dissolution now. And as the members no longer *have* to work, in fact barely lift a finger at all, many have left for a life of contemplation beyond these shores (not to tax havens, of course).

It is for this reason that any suggestions you might care to add to our records on time conversation can only be passed on with some difficulty. We therefore ask that any additional material should be accompanied by a small administration fee to the author who will place it in a special fund.

SUPER SCROOGE

3000 SNEAKY WAYS TO SAVE MONEY

MALCOLM STACEY

Now that you have digested *Superscrooge 2* you'll have plenty of spare time to sit back and enjoy *Superscrooge: 3000 sneaky ways to save money*. See some of the reviews at the front of this book. Available through all good bookshops or by sending the order form below direct to Quiller Press. Price £5.95 plus £1.00 postage and packing UK.

Quiller Press Limited
46 Lillie Road, London SW6 1TN

ORDER FORM

Please send me   copies of *Superscrooge: 3000 Sneaky Ways to Save Money*

I enclose my cheque for £   made out to QUILLER PRESS LTD.

or please charge my Access or Visa

No | | | | | | | | | | | | | | | | | |

Expiry date...

Name...

Address...

....

....

Signed...